…un, and adjective sentences

	Past		meaning
Positive	Negative		
生だった 生でした	学生　じゃ／では　なかった 学生　じゃ／では　ありませんでした 学生　じゃ／では　なかったです		*to be a student*
利だった 利でした	便利　じゃ／では　なかった 便利　じゃ／では　ありませんでした 便利　じゃ／では　なかったです		*convenient*
かった かったです	重くなかった 重くありませんでした 重くなかったです		*heavy*

…adjectives

…verbial f.	-te f.	-tara f.	-ba f.	meaning
	de	dattara	nara	
…に	学生で	学生だったら	学生なら	*to be a student*
利に	便利で	便利だったら	便利なら	*convenient*
	-kute	-kattara	-kereba	
…く	重くて 大きくて 安くて	重かったら 大きかったら 安かったら	重ければ 大きければ 安ければ	*heavy* *large* *cheap*
	よくて	よかったら	よければ	*good*

The shaded parts show the material covered in Volumes 1 and 2.

SITUATIONAL FUNCTIONAL JAPANESE

VOLUME *2*: NOTES
SECOND EDITION

TSUKUBA LANGUAGE GROUP

BONJINSHA CO.,LTD.

Published and distributed in Japan by BONJINSHA Co., Ltd.,
1F Ryoshin Hirakawacho Building, 1-3-13 Hirakawacho, Chiyoda-ku, Tokyo,
Telephone 03-3472-2240.
Printed in Singapore

First edition, 1992
Second edition, 1994   ISBN4-89358-254-2 C3081

CONTENTS

TABLE OF CONTENTS

Conversation Notes

⟨General Information⟩   ⟨Strategies⟩

1. Hospitals in Japan
2. Procedures in a hospital
3. Common phrases used by a doctor
4. Medicine

S-1. How to explain your symptoms
S-2. How to consult a doctor
S-3. How to ask for instructions on taking a medicine

---

1. Department stores in Japan
2. Expressions used in a department store
3. Colours, patterns, sizes of clothes

S-1. How to find what you want
S-2. How to ask for advice
S-3. How to decline politely

---

1. At a bookshop
2. Casual introductions

S-1. How to ask for something to be done for you —1.
S-2. How to order a book
S-3. How to cancel your order

---

1. Location and landmarks

S-1. How to ask for directions
S-2. How to give directions
S-3. How to go by public transport
S-4. How to confirm information —2.

B. Conversation

Lesson Title	Grammar Notes
L 13　喫茶店で At a coffee shop P.129〜154	Ⅰ. 好きだ／きらいだ／上手だ／下手だ Ⅱ. あげる／さしあげる 　　もらう／いただく ⎫ : giving and receiving〈1〉 　　くれる／くださる ⎭ Ⅲ. Noun modification〈2〉 Ⅳ. 〜している〈2〉: progressive action *V- ing* Ⅴ. 〜ばかりだ: *(only)just〜* Ⅵ. 〈quantity/duration〉＋も: *as many/long as*
L 14　忘れ物の問い合わせ Enquiring about a lost article P.155〜176	Ⅰ. Potential verbs Ⅱ. 〜て ⎰ あげる／さしあげる 　　　　⎱ もらう／いただく : giving and 　　　　　 くれる／くださる 　receiving〈2〉 Ⅲ. 〜に行く／来る (に〈6〉): *going/coming for〜* Ⅳ. 〈time〉までに　vs.　〈time〉まで
L 15　本を借りる Borrowing a book P.177〜202	Ⅰ. 〜てみる: to try doing Ⅱ. 〜ておく: do something for a future purpose Ⅲ. 〜てある: a state resulting from the action Ⅳ. 〜ていく: doing something and then going 　　〜てくる: doing something and then coming Ⅴ. Imperatives Ⅵ. 何か，だれか，どこか: 〈question word〉＋か 　　何も，だれも，どこも: 〈question word〉＋も Ⅶ. いつも，よく，ときどき，たまに，あまり， 　　めったに: adverbs of frequency Ⅷ. 〜中 (じゅう／ちゅう): *throughout〜, in the* 　　　　　　　　　　　　　　　*middle of〜*
L 16　電話をかける (2)： 　　　**タクシーを呼ぶ** 　　Phoning (2)： 　　Calling a taxi P.203〜226	Ⅰ. The -(y)oo form: plain form of 〜ましょう Ⅱ. 〜たり、〜たりする: indicating a range of 　　　　　　　　　　　　　　　activities Ⅲ. 〜し : indicating an addition Ⅳ. の〈3〉／こと: nominalizing a sentence Ⅴ. More on noun modification〈3〉
まとめ 4 (L 13〜16)	A. Grammar

Conversation Notes

〈General Information〉	〈Strategies〉
1. Introductions —3. 2. Building a relationship in a conversation	S-1. How to apologize and give an excuse S-2. How to confirm what you heard from someone S-3. How to bring up the main topic S-4. How to make and accept an offer S-5. How to express modesty
1. The lost-property office 2. Shape, colour and size	S-1. How to enquire about something you left behind S-2. How to answer questions S-3. How to confirm information —3. S-4. How to describe something S-5. How to express one's feelings
1. University libraries	S-1. How to start a conversation —6. After not having seen each other for a long time S-2. How to talk about other people S-3.·How to ask for advice on books S-4. How to thank for/decline offers of help S-5. How to ask how long you can borrow something
1. Using a taxi	S-1. How to propose a joint course of action S-2. How to substantiate a point with reasons S-3. How to call a taxi by phone S-4. How to explain where you are S-5. How to give instructions in a taxi

B. Conversation

This volume is the second of the three volume work, "Situational Functional Japanese." Preliminary explanation may be found in "How to Use This Book" in Volume 1. The table of contents of Volume 1 is shown below.

<Volume One>

TABLE OF CONTENTS

Conversation Notes

〈General Information〉   〈Strategies〉

1. Formal introductions   S-1. How to start a conversation —1.
2. Addressing people   At a party
3. Short questions and   S-2. How to introduce yourself or others
   responses   S-3. How to end a conversation —1.
4. *Aizuchi*   After a meeting

1. Post office services   S-1. How to start a conversation —2.
   in Japan   On the street
2. Letters and postcards   S-2. How to start a conversation —3.
3. Paying and receiving   Introducing a request
   money   S-3. How to send mail at the post office
                            S-4. How to buy something at the post
                                 office

1. At a restaurant   S-1. How to ask for something you need
2. Expressions used in   S-2. How to give and receive something
   restaurants and shops   S-3. How to order
3. Fast food shops   S-4. How to deal with problems in a
                                 restaurant
                            S-5. How to pay the cashier

1. Location   S-1. How to start a conversation —4.
                                 Introducing a question
                            S-2. How to ask the whereabouts of things/
                                 people
                            S-3. How to get something you didn't
                                 catch repeated
                            S-4. How to confirm information —1.
                            S-5. How to gain time to collect your
                                 thoughts
                            S-6. How to end a conversation —2. After
                                 asking a question

B. Conversation

Conversation Notes

⟨General Information⟩	⟨Strategies⟩
1. Katakana words	S-1. How to introduce a main topic —1.
	S-2. How to ask for information about a word
	S-3. How to make sure you have understood
	S-4. How to end a conversation —3. When the listener does not give the required explanation
1. Office instructions	S-1. How to introduce a main topic —2.
2. Delivery service	S-2. How to ask for instructions
	S-3. How to correct others' mistakes
	S-4. How to ask for advice implicitly
	S-5. How to give an alternative
1. Telephones	S-1. How to ask for a telephone number
2. Telephone numbers	S-2. How to make a telephone call
	S-3. How to deal with a wrong number
	S-4. How to introduce a question politely
	S-5. How to ask about office hours
	S-6. How to make an appointment
1. Relations between seniors and juniors in Japan	S-1. How to start a conversation —5. Asking for permission
	S-2. How to introduce a main topic —3.
2. A request for leave of absence	S-3. How to ask for permission
	S-4. How to give a warning

B. Conversation

Abbreviations and Notations

This is a list of main symbols used in this book:

	discourse particles
	structure particles
	connective particles
▼!	Be careful!
○	correct
×	wrong
[N]	noun
[A]	**-i** adjective
[NA]	**na** adjective
[V]	verb
[V(base)]	verb base
[V-(r)u]	**-(r)u** form of verb
[V-te]	**-te** form of verb
[V-ta]	**-ta** form of verb
[V-nai]	**-nai** form of verb
[V-nakatta]	**-nakatta** form of verb
《＋を verbs》	verb with を（object particle）
《－を verbs》	verb without を（object particle）
|S|	sentence
⇨	Refer
MC	Model Conversation
GN	Grammar Notes
CN	Conversation Notes
lit.	literally
Ⓕ	formal/polite speech
Ⓒ	casual/plain speech
⬆	speaking to a Higher
⬇	speaking to a Lower
➡	speaking to an Equal
♁	spoken by male
♁	spoken by female

第9課

病院で
びょういん
At a hospital

OBJECTIVES:

GRAMMAR

I. ～て〈2〉: connecting adjective and noun
    sentences
II. Reporting statements
    ～と言う（と〈3〉） : *say (s) that* ～
III. ～ので: *because* ～
IV. Adverbial use of **-i/na** adjectives
V. する verbs and なる verbs 〈2〉
VI. ***Keego*〈1〉「敬語」: irregular honorifics**
VII. ～だけ: *only* ～

CONVERSATION

＜General Information＞
1. Hospitals in Japan
2. Procedures in a hospital
3. Common phrases used by a doctor
4. Medicine

＜Strategies＞
S-1. How to explain your symptoms
S-2. How to consult a doctor
S-3. How to ask for instructions on taking a medicine

Model Conversation

Characters : Yamashita(山下), a receptionist(受付), a doctor(医者)

Situation : Yamashita-san is at the hospital reception. He fills in a form and explains that he has a fever and a sore throat. The doctor examines him and gives him some instructions.

Flow-chart :

Filling in the form	At the reception office
↓	
Waiting until being called	
↓	
Explaining your condition	In the consultation room
↓	
Consultation/Diagnosis	

―受付で―

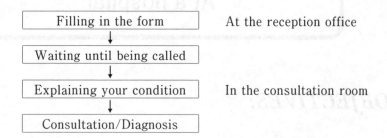

山　下　：すみません。

受　付　：はい。どうなさいました。

山　下　：あの、山下ですが……。

受　付　：あ、はい。ええ。山下さんですね。
　　　　　ええと、初診ですか。

山　下　：はい。

受　付　：それじゃ、こちらの用紙に記入してください。

山　下　：はい。

　　　　　＊　　　　　＊　　　　　＊

受　付　：ええと、保険証、お持ちですか。

山　下　：はい。

受　付　：じゃ、お名前、お呼びしますから、あちらでお待ちください。

山　下　：はい。

　　　　　＊　　　　　＊　　　　　＊

アナウンス：山下さん。山下和男さん。お入りください。

　　　　　＊　　　　　＊　　　　　＊

2

― 診察室で ―

山　下：失礼します。
医　者：どうぞかけてください。どうしました。
山　下：あの、きのうの朝からのどが痛くて。
医　者：うん。(Touching his throat)
山　下：熱もあるんです。
医　者：なるほど。おなかのほうは。
山　下：げりがひどいんです。
医　者：ああ、そうですか。

　　　　　　＊　　　＊　　　＊

医　者：じゃ、ちょっと熱をはかりましょう。

　　　　　　＊　　　＊　　　＊

医　者：(After a while) ３８度２分ありますね。
山　下：はあ。
医　者：口を大きく開けて。
山　下：あ……。(Opening his mouth)
医　者：じゃ、上だけぬいでください。
山　下：はい。
医　者：うしろ、向いて。
山　下：はい。
医　者：それじゃ、ちょっとそこに横になってください。(Pointing to a bed)
山　下：はい。(Lying on the bed)
医　者：ここ、痛いですか。(Pressing the abdomen)
山　下：いえ。
医　者：ここは。
山　下：はい、少し。あっ、痛っ！
医　者：はい、けっこうです。

*　　*　　*

医　者：かぜですね。

山　下：そうですか。

医　者：まあ、心配ないでしょう。

　　　　薬を出しますからね。薬局でもらってってください。

山　下：はい。どうもありがとうございました。

医　者：お大事に。

山　下：どうも。

Report

　日本の病院は、総合病院と医院があります。総合病院には、科がいろいろあります。コンピュータがたくさんあって、とても便利です。入院もできます。でも、患者が多いので、1時間から2時間ぐらい待ちます。

　医院は、ふつう、科が一つだけです。内科医院や眼科医院、歯科医院などにわかれています。かぜのときや、おなかが痛いときなどに行きます。

New Words and Expressions

Words in the conversation

受付	うけつけ	*reception*
医者	いしゃ	*doctor*
初診	しょしん	*one's first visit to a particular hospital*
用紙	ようし	*form*
記入する	きにゅうする	*to fill in*
保険証	ほけんしょう	*health insurance card*
呼ぶ	よぶ	*to call*
和男	かずお	*(male given name)*
診察室	しんさつしつ	*consultation room*
入る	はいる	*to enter*
かける		*to sit down*
のど		*throat*
痛い	いたい	*painful*
おなか		*stomach, abdomen*
～のほう		*what about ～*
げり		*diarrhea*
ひどい		*terrible*
はかる		*to measure, to take the temperature*
38度2分	38ど2ぶ	*38.2 degrees C*
口	くち	*mouth*
ぬぐ		*to take off one's clothes*
向く	むく	*to turn, to face*
横になる	よこになる	*to lie down*
薬	くすり	*medicine*
薬局	やっきょく	*pharmacy, drugstore*

<Expressions in the conversation>

どうなさいました。↗	*What's wrong?*
保険証、お持ちですか。	*Do you have a health insurance card?*

お持ちですか is polite for 持っていますか.

お呼びします。	*I'll call your name.*

Humble form of 呼ぶ. ⇨L18GN I

お入りください。	*Come in, please.*
お待ちください。	*Wait a moment, please.*

Honorific form of 待ってください. ⇨L10GN Ⅶ

なるほど。	*I see, really, indeed*
おなかのほうは。↗	*How about your tummy?*

ほう indicates a direction, side or area. There isn't much difference between おなかのほうは and おなかは, but 〜のほう is less direct and therefore polite.

38度2分	*38.2 degrees C (100.4 degrees F)*

In Japan, temperature is measured in centigrades. Normal body temperature is 36度5分; that's 98.6 degrees Fahrenheit. Body temperature is normally taken by placing a thermometer under the arm. 分 is a tenth of a degree of temperature. Note that the reading of 分 in this use is ぶ, not ふん.

上だけぬいでください。	*Take off your top.*
うしろ、向いて。↗	*Turn around. / Face the other way.*
横になってください。	*Lie down, please.*
はい、けっこうです。	*OK, that's it.*
もらってってください。	*Please get (your medicine from the pharmacy).*

This is a contracted form of 「もらっていってください。」. ⇨L15GN Ⅶ

心配はないでしょう。	*No need to worry.*

6

MC

Words in the report

総合病院	そうごうびょういん	*general hospital*
科	か	*department*
いろいろ（な）		*various*
便利（な）	べんり（な）	*convenient*
できる		*can, be able to*
患者	かんじゃ	*patient*
多い	おおい	*many*
～時間	～じかん	*～ hour(s)*
～ぐらい		*about ～*
内科	ないか	*internal medicine*
眼科	がんか	*opthalmology*
歯科	しか	*dentist*

\<Expressions in the report\>

ふつう	*generally*
おなかが痛いとき、	*when (you) have a stomach-ache* ⇨L20GNⅡ

Grammar Notes

Ⅰ．〜て〈2〉: connecting adjective and noun sentences

Examples

① 私の辞書は古くて、小さいです。　　*My dictionary is old and small.*
　わたし　じしょ　ふる　　ちい

② 田中さんは親切で、やさしいです。　　*Tanaka-san is helpful and kind.*
　たなか　　しんせつ

③ 鈴木さんは学生で、独身です。　　*Suzuki-san is a student and single.*
　すずき　　がくせい　どくしん

【*Explanation*】

1. [A-kute]、〜
　　[NA] de、〜

1) When two adjectives are used to describe some thing or person, they can be combined into one sentence by changing the first adjective into its **-te** form（[A-kute]/ [NA] de）:

> 私の辞書は ［古い＋小さい］
> 　　　　　　　　↓
> 私の辞書は 　古くて、小さいです。　　*My dictionary is old and small.*
>
> 田中さんは ［親切だ＋やさしい］
> 　　　　　　　　↓
> 田中さんは 　親切で、やさしいです。　　*Tanaka-san is helpful and kind.*

Note that the connective particle と, which connects nouns but never adjectives, cannot be used.

▼　　○　わたしの辞書は古くて、小さいです。
　　　　×　わたしの辞書は古いと小さいです。

2) Note that the two adjectives must be of similar meaning; if they express a contrast, they are linked instead by けど or が:

8

○　この本は高いですが、おもしろいです。
　　ほん　　たか
This book is expensive but interesting.

×　この本は高くて、おもしろいです。
(This book is expensive and interesting.)

　　This book is expensive and interesting, is unnatural, because *expensive* is normally a negative comment, whereas *interesting* is a positive one. Let's look at some further examples.

○　私のアパートは<u>きれいです</u>が、うるさいです。
　　わたし
My apartment is clean but noisy.

○　私のアパートは<u>きれいで</u>、静かです。
　　　　　　　　　　　　　　　　　しず
My apartment is clean and quiet.

×　私のアパートは<u>きれいで</u>、うるさいです。
(My apartment is clean and noisy.)

3）Two or more adjectives can also be joined with **-te** forms:

1. 宅急便は速くて、便利で、安い。
　　たっきゅうびん　はや　　　べんり　　やす
Takkyuubin is fast, convenient and cheap.

2. 鈴木さんはハンサムで、親切で、おもしろい。
　　すずき　　　　　　　　　　　しんせつ
Suzuki-san is handsome, helpful and interesting.

2. [N] de、〜

　　Two (or more) noun sentences can be connected with the **-te** from in the same way.

木村先生は ［この大学の先生だ＋私の指導教官だ］
きむらせんせい　　　　だいがく　　　　　　わたし　しどうきょうかん

木村先生はこの大学の先生で、私の指導教官だ。
Kimura-sensee is a teacher of this university and my academic adviser.

The -te form of adjectives		
	[A-i]	**[A-kute]**
[A]	**furui**　*old*	**furukute**

	omoshiroi *interesting* takai *high/expensive*	omoshirokute takakute
[NA]	[NA] da	[NA] de
	shinsetsu da *helpful* benri da *convenient*	shinsetsu de benri de

II. Reporting statements 〜と言う（と〈3〉）: *says (that)* 〜

Examples

① 山田さんは「3時に行きます」と言いました。
Yamada-san said, "I will be there at 3."

② 山田さんは3時に来ると言いました。
Yamada-san said that he'd come at 3.

③ 山田さんは「3時に行きます」と言っています。
Yamada-san says, "I will be there at 3."

④ 山田さんは3時に来ると言っています。
Yamada-san says that he'll come at 3.

⑤ 日本人は食事のとき「いただきます」と言います。
The Japanese say "Itadakimasu" at a meal.

【*Explanation*】

1. ⊲|||⊳∈ ： と〈3〉

The particle **と** indicates that the preceding sentence or words are a quotation.

2. Direct and indirect quotations

When reporting what someone (or yourself) has said, you can do this by using either a direct or an indirect quotation.

A direct quotation (① ③ and ⑤) simply repeats others' words; it is enclosed by the Japanese quotation marks 「　」 and followed by **と**.

In an indirect quotation (② and ④), the message is not repeated word for word, but rephrased from the current speaker's perspective. For this reason:

1) Polite forms are changed to plain forms (because only the CONTENT of the message is conveyed).

2) Unlike in English, the tense/mood of the predicate always remains the same.

<u>山田さんは 3 時に来ると言いました。</u>   *Yamada-san said that he'd come at 3.*
やまだ　　　　じ　　く　　　　　い
                non-past   past

3) Because the message is being related from the speaker's perspective, certain words may need to be changed. For example, **あなたのところに行きます** *(I'll) go to your place* becomes **私のところに来る** *(S/he)'ll come to my place.*
　　　　　　わたし

4) Quotation marks are not used.

1. 〈actual words〉 **山田：3 時に行きます。**

             Yamada：*I will be there at 3.*

        ↓

〈direct quotation〉 **山田さんは「3 時に行きます。」と言いました。**

             Yamada-san said, *"I'll be there at 3."*

〈indirect quotation〉 **山田さんは 3 時に来ると言いました。**

            Yamada-san said that he'd come at 3.

2. 〈actual words〉 **山下：シャルマさんは病気です。**
　　　　　　　　　　やました　　　　　　　　びょうき

        Yamashita：*Sharma-san is ill.*

        ↓

〈direct quotation〉 山下さんは「シャルマさんは病気です。」と言いました。
Yamashita-san said, "Sharma-san is ill."

〈indirect quotation〉 山下さんはシャルマさんは病気だと言いました。
Yamashita-san said that Sharma-san is/was ill.

3. 言いました versus 言っています

As you can see from ①〜④, both 言いました *said* and 言っています *says* can be used to convey others' words. As we saw in Lesson 8 about the difference between 〜た and 〜ている, if you simply focus on whether something was actually said or not, 言いました is used, but if you are concerned about the content of what was said (and the original statement has not yet been realized), 言っています is used. ⇨L8GNV

1. A：山田さんは何時に来るんですか。
   What time will Yamada-san come?

   B：山田さんは3時に来ると言っています。
   Yamada-san says that he'll come at 3.

2. A：3時までほんとうに待つんですか。
   Are we really going to wait (for him/her) until 3?

   B：ええ、3時まで待つと言いましたから。
   Yes, I told (him/her) that I'd wait until 3.

3. あなたは3時に来ると言いましたね。
   You said that you'd come at 3, didn't you?

〜って is often used in casual style with the meaning of 〜と言っています。

山田さんは3時に来るって。
Yamada-san says he'll come at 3.

4. 言います

言います is used to quote words that are spoken habitually, such as set phrases as in ⑤. It is also used with future actions.

1. 店の人は「いらっしゃいませ」と言います。(habitual)
   Shop attendants say (to customers)"Irasshaimase".

2. あした病院に行って、のどが痛いと言います。(future)
   Tomorrow I'll go to the hospital and tell (the doctor) that I have a sore throat.

Ⅲ. ⊕⊕ ～ので: *because* ～

GN

Examples

① 頭が痛かったので、病院へ行きました。
I went to the hospital because I had a headache.

② いっしょうけんめい勉強したので、よくわかりました。
I understood well because I studied hard.

③ あしたは休みなので、映画に行きます。
Tomorrow is my day off, so I'll go to the movies.

【*Explanation*】

1. The meaning of ので

Like {S₁}＋から（⇨L4GNⅢ）, {S₁}＋ので expresses a reason or cause, and {S₂} a result.

$$\boxed{\{S_1\}\ (\text{reason/cause})\ \text{ので}} + \boxed{\{S_2\}\ (\text{result})}$$

2. Comparing ～ので and ～から

There are several differences between ～ので and ～から:

1) The predicate preceding ので is usually in the plain（occasionally polite）form, whereas the predicate before から can be either the plain or the polite form.

2) から can be immediately followed by です, whereas ので cannot.

> A：どうして宿題をしませんでしたか。　*Why didn't you do the homework?*
>
> B：○ 頭が痛かったからです。　　*Because I had a headache.*
>
> 　　✕ 頭が痛かったのでです。

3) ～ので has a formal and objective ring, whereas ～から sounds casual and subjective.

3. The formation of ～ので clauses

When {S₁} is a non-past positive noun/**na** adjective sentence, だ（です）changes to **な** as indicated by * in the table below. For all others, the plain form is used at the end of {S₁}.

	reason	
[V]	食べる 食べた 食べない 食べなかった	
[A]	安い 安かった 安くない 安くなかった	ので
[NA]	静かな* 静かだった 静かじゃない 静かじゃなかった	+ result
[N]	休みな* 休みだった 休みじゃない 休みじゃなかった	ので

Ⅳ. Adverbial use of -i/na adjectives

Examples

① 口を大きくあけてください。
Please open your mouth wide.

② うるさいですね。静かに勉強してください。
You are (too) noisy! Study quietly.

【*Explanation*】

［A-ku］ and ［NA］＋ni function as adverbs.

大きい
おお
↓

口を 大きく あけました。
くち
(I) opened my mouth wide.

静かだ
しず
↓

静かに 勉強します。
べんきょう
(I) study quietly.

To form an adverb (modify a verb), change the final i of an -i adjective into ku and the da of a na adjective into ni:

1. 早く起きてください。（←早い）
   はや　お
   Please get up early.

2. きれいに書いてください。（←きれいだ）
   か
   Please write neatly (＝beautifully).

V. する verbs and なる verbs 〈2〉 ⇨L3GNⅢ

Examples

① 部屋をあたたかくしました。　　*I made the room warm (by making a fire).*
へや

② 部屋があたたかくなりました。　　*The room became warm.*

【*Explanation*】

Recall する *to make, to do,* and なる *to become.* An action or event can be presented in two ways:

(1) centering on the performer of the action
   (＝the person responsible for the action is explicit.)

(2) centering on the result of the action
   (＝the person responsible for the action is not explicit.)

する verbs are used for (1), while なる verbs are used for (2).

If we compare ① and ②, **あたたかくする** expresses the action of making a fire to warm the room, whereas **あたたかくなる** describes the natural course of events without specifying whether the room gets warmer naturally or as a result of someone taking action.

[A-ku] / [NA] に＋する, therefore, indicates an intentional action which causes a change, whereas [A-ku] / [NA] に＋なる indicates a natural change/result which may have been caused by someone, or may have happened naturally.

1. リサさんは部屋をきれいにしました。　　*Lisa-san cleaned the room.*
   (lit. Lisa-san made the room clean.)

   部屋がきれいになりました。　　*The room became clean.*

2. コーヒーを甘くしました。　　*I made the coffee sweet.*

   コーヒーが甘くなりました。　　*The coffee became sweet.*

VI. *Keego* 「敬語」〈1〉: irregular honorifics

--- **Examples** ---

① A：いつ日本にいらっしゃいましたか。　　*When did you come to Japan?*

B：先月来ました。　　*I came here last month.*

② A：どうぞ、めしあがってください。　　*Please eat.*

B：はい、ありがとうございます。　　*Yes, thank you very much.*

【*Explanation*】

So far, conversations have been either in the casual or formal style, as in the following examples: ⇨Introduction I

1) Conversation between friends

> A：ケーキ、食べる。↗
>
> B：うん、食べる。

2) Conversation between people who are not familiar with each other

> A：ケーキ、食べますか。
>
> B：ええ、食べます。

This lesson introduces *keego* 「敬語」, honorific and humble forms; *keego* can be used with either the casual or formal style of speech when dealing with a Higher. Let us look first at honorific expressions: ⇨Introduction I, L18GN I for humble expressions.

鈴木さん will normally use casual speech when speaking to a junior (シャルマさん, リサさん, or 田中さん) or to a close friend of about the same age/year; however, when addressing a Higher, 木村先生, he will use formal speech combined with honorific forms: ⇨L8CN I

鈴木さん
すずき

木村先生（Suzuki's Higher）
きむらせんせい

3）Honorific

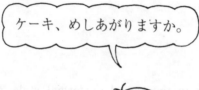

鈴木：ケーキ、めしあがりますか。　　*Would you like to eat some cake?*
先生：はい、食べます。　　　　　　　*Yes, I would.*
　　　　　　た

⇨Introduction I, L10GN Ⅶ, L18GN I, L19GN Ⅳ

Honorific forms are normally used when the listener（or the person spoken about）is a Higher; Highers include senior students, teachers and older people, as well as people you do not know very well.

There are three types of honorific forms:

（1）Irregular honorifics
（2）Regular honorifics　　　⇨L10GN Ⅶ
（3）Passive honorifics　　　⇨L19GN Ⅳ

Overleaf, let us look at some verbs with irregular honorific forms.

GN

いる	to stay	いらっしゃる／いらっしゃいます*
行く	to go	おいでになる／おいでになります
来る	to come	
食べる	to eat	めしあがる／めしあがります
飲む	to drink	
言う	to say	おっしゃる／おっしゃいます*
見る	to see	ごらんになる／ごらんになります
〜ている		〜ていらっしゃる／〜ていらっしゃいます ex. 住んでいらっしゃいます　to live 　　持っていらっしゃいます　to have
する	to do	なさる／なさいます*
〜する		（ご／お）** 〜 なさる／なさいます* ex.（お）料理なさいます　to cook 　　（ご）結婚なさいます　to get married

*　The polite forms of いらっしゃる, おっしゃる, なさる, etc. are いらっしゃいます,
おっしゃいます, and なさいます.

1．A：いつ日本にいらっしゃいましたか。　　*When did you come to Japan?*

　　B：先月来ました。　　*I came last month.*

2．A：あした京都にいらっしゃいますか。　　*Will you go to Kyoto tomorrow?*

　　B：はい、行きます。　　*Yes, I will.*

3．どうぞ、めしあがってください。　　*Please eat.*

4．先生がそうおっしゃいました。　　*Our teacher said so.*

5．林さんは横浜に住んでいらっしゃいます。　　*Hayashi-san lives in Yokohama.*

** ご／お is optional.

6．A：いつ（ご）結婚なさいますか。　　*When will you get married?*
　　　 けっこん

　 B：来年結婚します。　　　　　　　*I'll get married next year.*
　　　らいねん

Below are some examples of verbal nouns that can be used with **ご** or **お**. ⇨L1CN1

ご＋ verbal noun		**お＋ verbal noun**	
結婚する	*to get married*	電話する	*to telephone*
		でん わ	
説明する	*to explain*	洗濯する	*to do the laundry*
せつめい		せんたく	
相談する	*to consult*	掃除する	*to clean*
そうだん		そうじ	
連絡する	*to contact*	料理する	*to cook*
れんらく		りょう り	

Some verbal nouns take neither **ご** nor **お**.

運転する　　　　　*to drive*
うんてん

テニスする　　　　*to play tennis*

7．林 さんは 車 を運転なさいません。　*Hayashi-san doesn't drive a car.*
　 はやし　　 くるま

8．A：テニスなさいますか。　　　　　*Do you play tennis?*

　 B：ええ、少しします。　　　　　　*Yes, I play a little.*
　　　　　すこ

Ⅶ. ～だけ: *only* ～

[N] **だけ** is used to indicate a limit (*just, only*):

1．シャツだけ（を）ぬぎました。　　*(I) took off just the shirt (no more).*

2．切手は１０まいだけ買いました。　*As for stamps, I bought just ten (no*
　 きって　　　　　　　 か　　　　*more).*

3．山田さんだけ（が）欠席しています。*Only Yamada-san is absent.*
　 やまだ　　　　　　けっせき

You will notice that **が** and **を** are often omitted in casual speech.

Conversation Notes

<General Information>

1. Hospitals in Japan

a. Private Hospitals (**医院**)
いいん

The private hospital or clinic you will find in your neighbourhood is the place to go for common illnesses like a cold or a stomachache. Most private hospitals hold office hours on a first come, first served basis. They are not normally equipped with the latest medical machinery, though. When a patient's condition is serious, the doctor will therefore refer him to a general hospital.

b. General hospitals (**総合病院**)
そうごうびょういん

General hospitals are equipped to take care of most types of illness. Office hours are usually held during the morning on selected weekdays, so it is advisable to check a department's consultation time before going to the hospital. For hospitalized patients, general hospitals provide bed and bedding, but patients are expected to bring their own pajamas and towels, etc.

Hospital visiting hours are generally in the afternoon till about 6 p.m.. Visitors are often required to sign in and out. (⇨L22)

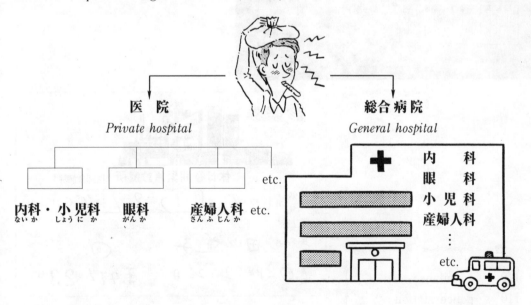

医 院
Private hospital

内科・小児科　眼科　　産婦人科 etc.
ないか　しょうにか　がんか　さんふじんか

総合 病院
General hospital

内　科
眼　科
小児科
産婦人科
⋮
etc.

<Hospital departments>

内科	ないか	*internal medicine*
外科	げか	*surgery*
小児科	しょうにか	*pediatrics*
産婦人科	さんふじんか	*obstetrics and gynecology*
整形外科	せいけいげか	*orthopedics*
皮膚科	ひふか	*dermatology*
泌尿器科	ひにょうきか	*urology*
眼科	がんか	*opthalmology*
耳鼻科	じびか	*ear and nose department*
歯科	しか	*dentistry*
放射線科	ほうしゃせんか	*radiology*

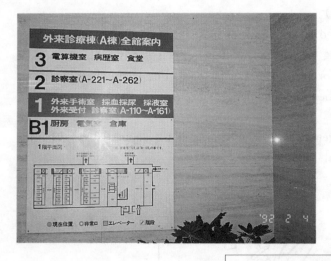

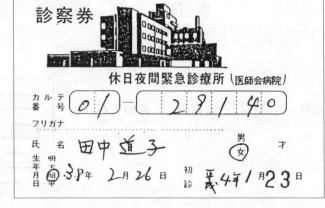

☎		
119	ambulance	
110	police station	

2. Procedures in a hospital

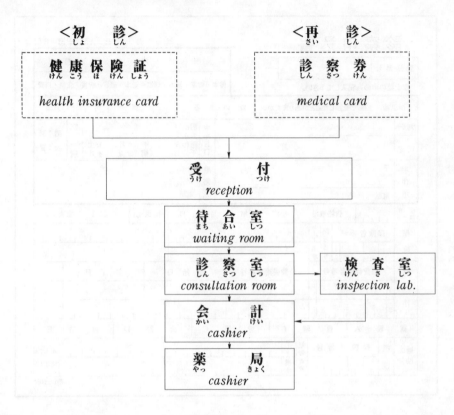

When a patient comes to a hospital for the first time, the receptionist will ask:

| はじめてですか。 | *Are you a new patient?* |
| 初診ですか。 | |

When coming to a hospital for the first time, you need to show your National Health Insurance card at the reception. Generally, any foreigner who plans to stay in Japan for more than one year can join the National Health Insurance scheme, under which only 30% of the medical service charge has to be paid by the patient. It is especially advisable to join if you bring your family to Japan.

At the reception you will have to fill out an application form, but if you find it difficult to write in Japanese, the receptionist will help you to fill it out.　⇨CD3

In some general hospitals you have to fill out medical history forms 受診（じゅしん）カードat the reception desk of each department. This form gathers data about the patient before s/he consults a doctor. Questions such as what health problems s/he has, what medication s/he takes, etc. are included.

New words and instructions on the form:

診察申込書

登録番号 ☐☐☐☐☐☐☐

※太線の中のみ記入して下さい。

年　　月　　日　AM PM 夜間

循・脳・消・内・外・小・整・形

健本・健家・国本・国家・退本・退家・労災・生保・自費

| ※以前、当院で受診したことがありますか。 | な い・あ る　　　　科　　　年　　　月頃 |

フリガナ

氏名

生年月日　明治M　大正T　昭和S　平成H　年　月　日生（満　才　ヶ月）

性別　男：M　女：F

現住所　〒　電話　（　　）

勤務先　電話　（　　）

住所コード　資格取得　平成　年　月　日　未 提 出　本人：1　家族：2

保険　保険者番号　記号番号　コード漢字

諸法　公費負担者番号　公費受給者番号　開 始 日　終 了 日

1
2

継 続 A　自 賠 B　労 災 C　公 災 D　自 費 E

補助区分　継続　保 険 者 番 号　記号番号　コード漢字　本人：1　家族：2

KMC 1004

| 診察申込書 | しんさつもうしこみしょ | *application form for medical examination* |
| 太線の中のみ記入して下さい。 ふとせん なか きにゅう | | *Fill in only the sections within the bold line.* |

循・脳・消・内・外・小・整・形

循＝循環器科	じゅんかんきか	*circulatory department*
脳＝脳外科	のうげか	*brain department*
消＝消化器科	しょうかきか	*digestive department*
内＝内科	ないか	*internal medicine department*
外＝外科	げか	*surgery department*
小＝小児科	しょうにか	*pediatrics department*
整＝整形外科	せいけいげか	*orthopedics department*
形＝形成外科	けいせいげか	*plastic surgery department*

24

以前、当院で受診したことがありますか。 *Have you ever had a medical check in this hospital, before?*

以前	いぜん	*before*
当院	とういん	*this hospital*
受診	じゅしん	*have a medical check*
フリガナ		*small kana giving kanji readings*
氏名	しめい	*name*
生年月日	せいねんがっぴ	*date of birth*
明治	めいじ	*Meiji Era*（1868-1912）
大正	たいしょう	*Taisho Era*（1912-1926）
昭和	しょうわ	*Showa Era*（1926-1989）
平成	へいせい	*Heisei Era*（1989-　　）

Since the Meiji Era, the period of an emperor's reign has been used as the standard way to indicate the year, including the year of one's birth（e.g. Showa 40 is 1965）. The present era is called Heisei and began in 1989. Nowadays, official documents are still dated with the Japanese era year, but the Western calender is also widely used.

満	まん	*age (used with years)*
性別	せいべつ	*sex*
現住所	げんじゅうしょ	*current address*
勤務先	きんむさき	*name and address of employer*

3．Common phrases used by a doctor

When a doctor asks a patient about his symptoms, he will often say:

どうしました。↗ 　　　　　　　　*What's wrong?*
どうかしましたか。

「どうなさいましたか。」is the polite equivalent of「どうしましたか。」. In the model conversation, the receptionist politely asked Yamashita-san「どうなさいましたか。」. However, a Japanese male doctor tends to use plain language to his patients, so he may say「どうしたの。↗」，「どうしました。↗」or「どうしたんですか。」.

Other common phrases:

上だけぬいでください。
Take off your top (shirt, blouse etc.), please.

うしろをむいてください。
Turn around, please.

そこに横になってください。
Lie down there, please.

ここは、どうですか。
How about here, please?

あおむけになってください。
Lie on your back, please.

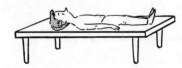

うつぶせになってください。
Lie face down, please.

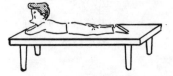

口を大きく開けて。↗
Open wide, please.

息をとめて。↗
Hold your breath, please.

4. Medicine

After the examination, the doctor will often give you a prescription. It is advisable to ask the doctor what it is that he is prescribing you, and when and how often you need to take it. Some medicines, including aspirin （アスピリン） and other mild painkillers（**痛みどめ，いたみどめ**）cold cures（**かぜ薬，かぜぐすり**）and vitamins（**ビタミン剤，ビタミンざい**）are available without prescription. These you can get at a pharmacy.

Prescriptions often need not be taken to a pharmacy because many hospitals and clinics have their own in-house pharmacy where the medicine will be made up for you.

The sheet below is an instruction for a week's supply of medicine to be taken three times a day（after meals），consisting of one pouch of pulverized medicine and one pill to be taken each time.

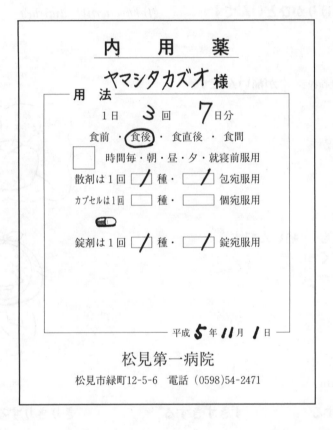

Types of medicine:

散剤	さんざい	*a powder*
カプセル		*capsule*
錠剤	じょうざい	*a tablet*

<Strategies>

S-1. How to explain your symptoms

~んです is useful for explaining one's symptoms, for example:

① **頭が痛いんです。** *(I) have a headache.*
  あたま いた

② **げりがひどいんです。** *(I) have terrible diarrhea.*

a. Pain

＜part of body＞	
頭	が痛いんです。
歯は	
おなか	
ここ	

b. Degree of pain

とても	痛いんです。
すごく	
少し	
すこ	

c. Type of pain

がんがんする	**ずきずきする**	**きりきりする**
a splitting headache	*a throbbing pain*	*a biting pain*

  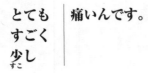

CN

d. General symptoms

むかむかする
to feel like vomiting
to feel nauseous

くらくらする
to feel dizzy

だるい
to feel a lack of energy

e. Other explations of symptoms.

足をひねる	*to sprain one's foot*
足をおる	*to break one's foot*
やけどをする	*to get burnt*
指を切る	*to cut one's finger*

S-2.　How to consult a doctor

To ask the doctor if you are permitted to do something you can use [**V-te**] も
いいですか. ⇨L8GNⅦ

① **patient** ：**お酒を飲んでもいいでしょうか。**
　　　　　　　Is it all right to drink alcohol?

　doctor ：**いいえ。お酒は、いけませんよ。**
　　　　　　　No, you shouldn't take any alcohol.

② **patient** ：**運動してもいいですか。**
　　　　　　　Is it all right to do exercise?

　doctor ：**そうですね。↘　できるだけ、静かに休んでください。**
　　　　　　　Hmm. Try to rest as much as possible.

To ask permission for not doing something, use 〜なくてもいいですか.

① 入院しなくてもいいでしょうか。
にゅういん
Would it be all right not to enter hospital?

② 手術をしなくてもいいでしょうか。
しゅじゅつ
Is it all right not to have an operation?

③ アレルギーがあるので、この薬を飲まなくてもいいですか。
くすり の
I'm allergic to this medicine. Is it all right not to take it?

S-3. How to ask for instructions on taking a medicine

In Japanese hospitals, medication is often not explained to the patient in detail. Therefore it is advisable to find out more about your medicine by asking questions.

If you are unsure what type of medicine you are given you can ask the doctor or nurse (看護婦, かんごふ) as follows:

これは、何の薬ですか。
なん
What kind of medicine is this?/What is this medicine for?

To find out when and how often you need to take the medicine, ask:

この薬は、いつ、何回飲みますか。
なんかい
When and how often do I have to take this medicine?

If you are allergic to certain medications you can say:

(…) のアレルギーがあるんです。
I am allergic to (...).

できれば、薬を飲みたくないんですが。
If possible, I'd rather not take any medicine.

30

第10課

デパートで

At a department store

OBJECTIVES:

GRAMMAR

- Ⅰ. Noun modification 〈1〉
- Ⅱ. の〈2〉: ~ *one*
- Ⅲ. Comparison
- Ⅳ. ~は ~が + adjective
- Ⅴ. ~というのは: for unfamiliar topics
- Ⅵ. ~さ: nouns derived from adjectives
- Ⅶ. *Keego*「敬語」〈2〉: regular honorifics

CONVERSATION

＜General Information＞

1. Department stores in Japan
2. Expressions used in a department store
3. Colours, patterns and sizes of clothes

＜Strategies＞

- S-1. How to find what you want
- S-2. How to ask for advice
- S-3. How to decline politely

Model Conversation

Characters : Yamashita(山下), a customer(客), an elevator operator(エレベーター), a shop assistant(店員)

Situation : Yamashita-san goes to a department store. He goes up to the 5th floor by elevator and looks for a large-sized sweater. A young shop assistant helps him select one.

Flow-chart :

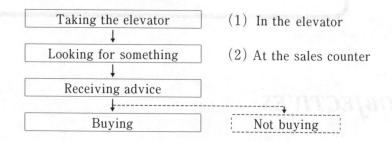

Taking the elevator	(1) In the elevator
↓	
Looking for something	(2) At the sales counter
↓	
Receiving advice	
↓----------------→	
Buying	Not buying

（1）―エレベーターで―

エレベーター：ご来店くださいまして、ありがとうございます。
　　　　　　　上へまいります。
　　　　　　　ご利用階数をお知らせくださいませ。
客　　　　　：3階、お願いします。
エレベーター：3階、かしこまりました。
　　　　　　　おあと、ございませんか。
山　下　　　：すみません。5階、お願いします。
エレベーター：5階、かしこまりました。上へまいります。

　　　　　　　＊　　　＊　　　＊

エレベーター：次は5階へまいります。紳士服、紳士用品の売り場でございます。
　　　　　　　お待たせいたしました。5階でございます。

（2）―売り場で―

山　下：すみません。
店　員：はい。いらっしゃいませ。
山　下：大きいサイズのセーター、ありますか。
店　員：はい。こちらにございます。
山　下：ええと、このLLっていうのは、ぼくには大きいかな。

32

MC

店　員：そうですね。メーカーによってもちがいますから、どうぞお試しください。
山　下：あの、試着室は。
店　員：はい。あの、あちらにございます。
山　下：ああ、どうも。

　　　　　＊　　　＊　　　＊

店　員：いかがでございますか。
山　下：ええと、この色で無地の、ありませんか。
店　員：はい。じゃあ、こちらなどはいかがでしょう。
山　下：もう少し明るい色のほうがいいんですけど。
店　員：それでは、こちらは。
山　下：ううん……。色はいいんですけど、デザインがちょっとね。

　　　　　＊　　　＊　　　＊

店　員：こちらは、最近流行の形ですが。
山　下：そうですね。こっちのほうがいいかな。
　　　　じゃあ、これをください。
店　員：ありがとうございます。8000円になります。
山　下：はい。
店　員：1万円おあずかりいたします。少々お待ちください。

　　　　　＊　　　＊　　　＊

店　員：お待たせいたしました。2000円のおかえしでございます。
山　下：どうも。
店　員：どうもありがとうございました。

Report

＜日　記＞
10月14日（金）
　きょうは一人でデパートへ行った。大きさがわからなかったので店員に聞いて、一番大きいサイズのセーターを買った。無地でじみな色のセーターだ。もう少し明るい色のほうがよかったが、店員が最近流行のデザインだと言ったので、それにした。ちょっとかわいい店員だった。

New Words and Expressions

Words in the conversation

客	きゃく	customer
エレベーター		elevator, lift
店員	てんいん	shop assistant
まいる		to go, to come
		humble for 行く and 来る
知らせる	しらせる	to inform, to let know
次	つぎ	next
紳士服	しんしふく	men's wear
紳士用品	しんしようひん	men's goods
売り場	うりば	sales counter
サイズ		size
セーター		sweater
L L		extra large ＝ X L
メーカー		maker, manufacturer
ちがう		to differ, to be different
試す	ためす	to try
試着室	しちゃくしつ	fitting room
いかが		how? ＝ polite form of どう
色	いろ	colour
無地	むじ	plain, no pattern
もう少し	もうすこし	a little more
明るい	あかるい	light, bright
それでは		in that case
デザイン		design
最近	さいきん	recently
流行	りゅうこう	in fashion, popular
		cf. 流行する to be in fashion
形	かたち	shape, form

＜*Expressions in the conversation*＞

ご来店くださいまして、ありがとうございます。
_{らいてん}

Thank you very much for coming to this store. ⇨CN2

上へまいります。
_{うえ}

Going up. ⇨CN2

まいる is *humble* for 行く（*to go*）and 来る（*to come*）. ⇨L18GN I
_い

ご利用階数をお知らせくださいませ。
_{りようかいすう}　　　　し

Which floor, sir/madam?

お＋［Verb(base)］＋ください。⇨GN Ⅶ

3階、お願いします。
_{がい}　_{ねが}

3rd floor, please.

かしこまりました。

Certainly, sir/madam.

Polite way of expressing わかりました. ⇨CN2

おあと、ございませんか。

Any other floors?

ございます is *humble* for ある *(to have, to exist).* ⇨L18GN I

お待たせいたしました。
_ま

Sorry to have kept you waiting.

このLLっていうのは、ぼくには大きいかな。
_{おお}

Is this LL (＝XL) size too large for me, I wonder.

〜って ⇨GN V

メーカーによってもちがいますから。

Because (the size) differs according to the maker.

どうぞあちらでお試しください。
_{ため}

Please try it on over there. ⇨GN Ⅶ, CN2

いかがでございますか。

How do you find it?/What do you think? ⇨CN2

こちらなどはいかがでしょう。

How do you like this one?

など means *and the like*; here it is used to make the suggestion more indirect and polite. Note that it is different from など in L4GN V.

〜のほうがいいんですけど。

(I) prefer 〜./(I) like 〜 better. ⇨GN Ⅲ

〜のほうがいい ⇨GN Ⅲ/〜けど ⇨CN S-3

色はいいんですけど、デザインがちょっとね。
_{いろ}
(I) like the colour, but the design is a bit...

こっちのほうがいいかな。

Is this one better, I wonder.

Words in the report

日記	にっき	*diary*
金	きん	＝金曜日（きんようび）*Friday*
デパート		*department store*
大きさ	おおきさ	*size*
一番	いちばん	*the most, the best*
じみ（な）		*subdued, plain*
ちょっと		*a little*
かわいい		*cute, charming*

Grammar Notes

I．Noun modification ⟨1⟩

Examples

① A：どんなセーターを買ったんですか。 *What kind of sweater did you buy?*

   B：赤いセーターを買ったんです。 *I bought a red sweater.*

② きれいなセーターを買いたいんです。 *I want to buy a beautiful sweater.*

③ みどりのセーターを買います。 *I will buy a green sweater.*

【Explanation】

1. The function of noun modification

Adjectives or nouns can be used to modify nouns, describing in more detail the noun they precede:

[A-i] ＋ [N]

赤いセーター　　　　　　 *a red sweater*
大きいサイズ　　　　　　 *a large size*
おもしろい雑誌　　　　　 *an interesting magazine*

[NA] な ＋ [N]

きれいなセーター　　　　 *a beautiful sweater*
まじめな学生　　　　　　 *a serious-minded student*
親切な人　　　　　　　　 *a helpful person*

[N] の ＋ [N]　⇨L1GNⅣ

みどりのセーター　　　　 *a green sweater*

2. どんな as noun modifier

どんな ＋ ［N］		*what kind of* ［N］ *?*

To ask about the characteristics of a noun, simply use the question word **どんな** as a modifier, as in ①.

1. A：田中さんはどんな人ですか。 *What sort of a person is Tanaka-san?*

   B：かわいい人です。 *(She's) a charming person.*

2. A：どんなセーターがいいですか。 *What sort of sweater do you like?*

   B：赤いセーターがいいです。 *I like red sweaters.*

3. A：どんなデザインがいいですか。 *What sort of design do you like?*

   B：流行のデザインがいいです。 *I like fashionable designs.*

3. Grammatical function of the modifier ＋ noun sequence

The combination **modifier ＋ ［N］** as a whole functions like a noun:

大きいサイズのセーターを買いました。
(I) bought a large-sized sweater.

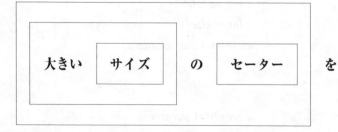

［N］phrase　　　　　　　　　　　　　　　　［V］

大きい　サイズ　の　セーター　を　買いました。

4. Types of colour words

There are two types of colour words in Japanese; words like **みどり** *green* and **むらさき** *purple* are nouns and have no adjective form, whereas **白い** *white* and **赤い** *red* etc. are **-i** adjectives. The stem (the form minus the final **い**) of adjective colour words is sometimes used as a noun which indicates the name of the colour:

みどりのセーター 　　*a green sweater*
白いセーター 　　*a white sweater*
白のセーター 　　*a sweater of white color*

The noun form is also used in questions and answers concerned with identifying the colour of something:

> A：リサさんのセーターはどんな色
> 　ですか。
> *What colour is Lisa -san's sweater?*
>
> B：○　赤です。
> *It's red.*
>
> 　　×　赤いです。

Ⅱ. の〈2〉: ～ *one*

Examples

① A：テレビ、ありますか。
　　Do you have a TV?

　 B：ええ、先週 新しいのを買いました。
　　Yes, I bought a new one last week.

② A：これは田中さんの本ですか。
　　Is this Tanaka-san's book?

　 B：いえ、山田さんのです。
　　No, it's Yamada-san's.

【*Explanation*】

の can be used in place of a noun that is understood from the context. In ① 新しいの is used instead of 新しいテレビ, thus avoiding repetition of the noun テレビ. 山田さんの in ② means *Yamada-san's*, i.e 本 is dropped to avoid being repetitive.

新しい辞書	→新しいの	*a new dictionary/a new one*
古い本	→古いの	*an old book/an old one*
きれいなくつ	→きれいなの	*beautiful shoes/beautiful ones*
私の本	→私の	*my book/mine*
田中さんのペン	→田中さんの	*Tanaka-san's pen/Tanaka-san's*

Ⅲ. Comparison

Examples

① A：このセーターとあのセーターと、どちら（のほう）が安いですか。
   Which is cheaper, this sweater or that one?

   B：このセーターのほうが安いです。　*This sweater is cheaper.*

② 階段よりエレベーターのほうが便利です。
   The elevator is more convenient than the stairs.

③ エレベーターは階段より便利です。
   The elevator is more convenient than the stairs.

④ A：山下さんと田中さんとどちらがたくさん買いましたか。
   Who bought more, Yamashita-san or Tanaka-san?

   B：田中さんのほうがたくさん買いました。*Tanaka-san bought more.*

⑤ A：この中で、どれがいちばん安いですか。
   Which is the cheapest among these?

   B：それが（一番）安いです。／それです。
   That one is the cheapest.　　／That one.

【*Explanation*】

1. The structure of comparative sentences

The structure used for comparative sentences is as below:

A ＜thing/person/place/etc.＞　のほうが
B ＜thing/person/place/etc.＞　より

＞ predicate

→このセーターのほうがあのセーターより安い。
→あのセーターよりこのセーターのほうが安い。
   This sweater is cheaper than that one.

40

You can use either

AのほうがBより＜predicate＞, or
BよりAのほうが＜predicate＞.

Both mean *A is more ＜predicate＞ than B.*

ほう (grammatically speaking a noun) indicates that **A** is the choice between the two alternatives offered. To make **A** the topic of the sentence, use **A は** instead of **A の ほうが** (③). **より** in a comparative sentence corresponds to English *than.*

2. Comparative questions

To ask about a choice of alternatives, (① and ④), use:

> [N] と [N] と、どちら（のほう）が　predicate

1. A：愛とお金とどちらのほうが大切ですか。
   あい　かね　　　　　　　たいせつ
   Which is more important, love or money?

   B：両方 大切です。／どちらも大切です。
   りょうほう
   Both are important.

2. みどりのと白のと、どちらのほうがいいですか。
   しろ
   Which is better, the green one or the white one?

When [N] consists of ＜adjective＋の＞ (ex. 大きいの　小さいの), 小さいほ
　　　　　　　　　　　　　　　　　　　　　　　　おお　　　　ちい
う is normally used instead of **小さいののほう**:

3. A：大きいのと小さいのと、どちらがいいですか。
   Which would you like, the big one or the little one?

   B：小さい（のの）ほうがいいです。
   I'd like the little one.

3. Comparing three or more items

To compare three or more items (⑤), use:

> \<group name\>　（の中）で、［N］　が　一番　predicate
> 　　　　　　　　　　なか　　　　　　　　いちばん

1. 家族の中で、母が一番忙しいです。
　　か ぞく　　　はは　　いちばん いそが

Mother is the busiest (person) in my family.

In the following example, a place name is used like a group name as the topic of the sentence.

2. 日本（の中）では、富士山が一番高い。
　　に ほん　　　　　　ふ じ さん　　いちばんたか

In Japan, Mt. Fuji is the highest (mountain).

4. Asking about three or more items

> \<group name\>　（の中）で、\<question word\>　が　一番　predicate

1. お酒の中で、どれが一番強いですか。
　　さけ　　　　　　　　いちばんつよ

Which is the strongest alcoholic drink?

(lit. Which is the strongest among alcoholic drinks?)

2. 日本の食べ物（の中）で、何が一番おいしいですか。
　　に ほん た　もの　　　　　なに　いちばん

What is the most delicious of Japanese dishes?

Note that you cannot use どちら／どっち because these indicate only a choice between two alternatives. To compare three or more items, use どれ (thing), 何 (thing), だれ(person), どこ(place), いつ(time) , etc.

Both どれ and 何 are used to compare things, but どれ *which* is used when the items compared are specific or countable. When the items compared are non-specific or general, 何 *what* is used. For example, in 1. a choice is made from several varieties of alcoholic drink, such as whisky, wine and beer. In the second example the group referred to cannot be counted (there is an unlimited number of dishes in Japanese food), so 何 is used.

In the above structure, ［N］と［N］と［N］ can also be used instead of the group name:

3. **ひらがなとかたかなと漢字の中で、漢字が一番おもしろい。**

Among hiragana, katakana, and kanji, kanji are the most interesting.

4. **ジュースとお茶とコーヒーのうちで、どれが一番飲みたいですか。**

Of juice, green tea, and coffee, which do you want to drink most?

うちで can be used instead of **中で**.

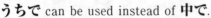

IV. : **〜は〜が ＋ adjective**

Examples

① **このセーターは色がいいです。**

The colour of this sweater is nice.

(lit. As for this sweater, the colour is nice.)

② **このセーターは色はいいけど、デザインが悪い。**

This sweater has a nice colour but is bad in design.

(lit. As for this sweater, the colour is good but the design is bad.

【Explanation】

1. Describing the characteristics of a thing/person

The characteristics of something, for instance a sweater, **セーター**, can be described in a variety of ways: in terms of its colour, size, price, or design. In ①, the speaker describes **このセーター** *this sweater* in terms of its colour, commenting that it is nice.

Below are some more sentences commenting in a variety of ways on the same topic:

43

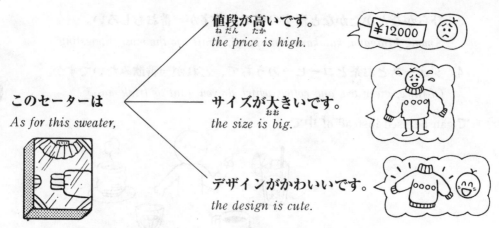

値段が高いです。
the price is high.

このセーターは
As for this sweater,

サイズが大きいです。
the size is big.

デザインがかわいいです。
the design is cute.

Here are some further examples with the same sentence structure:

1. あの人は背が高い。
   That person is tall.
   (lit. As for that person, his stature is tall.)

2. 田中さんはかみが長い。
   Tanaka-san has long hair.
   (lit. As for Tanaka-san, her hair is long.)

2. 🐟 : the contrastive use of は

Here are some sentences with contrastive は: ⇨ まとめ2A Ⅶ

1. 田中さんは買いましたが、鈴木さんは買いませんでした。
   Tanaka-san bought (something), but Suzuki-san didn't.

2. （私は）チキンは食べますが、ポークは食べません。
   I eat chicken but I don't eat pork.

3. 電話は、田中さんにはかけましたが、鈴木さんにはかけませんでした。
   I phoned Tanaka-san, but not Suzuki-san.

When you comment on a positive aspect of a sweater using は rather than が（このセーターは色はいいけど…）, the implication is that you feel that it has shortcomings in some other respect. Likewise, commenting negatively on some aspect using は implies that there is also something good about it.

Such contrasts can also be expressed fully, as in the following sentences (to emphasize the second item, use が rather than は):

4. 日本語は、ひらがなはやさしいけど、漢字がむずかしいです。
   In Japanese, Hiragana are easy, but Kanji are difficult.

5. この大学は、キャンパスはせまいが、図書館が大きい。
   The campus of this university is small, but the library is big.

Ⅴ. ～というのは: for unfamiliar topics

Compare the following two sentences.

① 漢字はむずかしいです。　　　　*Kanji are difficult.*
　　かんじ

② 漢字というのはむずかしいです。　　*What we call Kanji are difficult.*

① uses a structure you are familiar with from Lesson 6; the speaker makes his comment on Kanji in this way because he assumes that the listener knows what Kanji are. [N] というのは is used instead of [N] は when the speaker assumes that listener is unfamiliar with the word Kanji, as in ②.

Likewise, a speaker will use this structure to ask about a topic whose meaning is not clear:

1. LL というのは、どのぐらいの大きさですか。
　　　　　　　　　　　　　　　　　おお
　　How big is what you call 'LL'?

2. A：なっとうというのは何ですか。
　　　　　　　　　　　　　なん
　　What is this stuff they call 'nattoo'?

B：日本の食べ物です。
　　にほん　た　もの
　　It's a Japanese food.

[N] っていうのは or [N] って are often used colloquially instead of [N] というのは. ⇨L5CN S-2 まとめBⅡ

A：なっとうって、何ですか。

B：なっとうっていうのは、日本の食べ物です。

The meaning of a word which is unfamiliar to the listener can be explained with a familiar term using the following structure:

[N] (unfamiliar) というのは [N] (familiar) のことだ

1. ワープロというのはワードプロセッサのことです。
　　'Waapuro' is 'word-processor'.

2. 領収書というのはレシートのことです。
　　りょうしゅうしょ
　　'Ryooshuusho' is 'receipt'.

Ⅵ. ～さ: nouns derived from adjectives

The suffix －さ can be attached to the stem of an adjective to make it into a noun, as illustrated below:

広さ	*width*	←広い
長さ	*length*	←長い
重さ	*weight*	←重い
大きさ	*size*	←大きい
高さ	*height/costliness*	←高い
強さ	*strength*	←強い
深さ	*depth*	←深い

A：その本の大きさはどのぐらい*ですか。
What's the size of the book?

B：このぐらいです。
About this.

*どのぐらい *about what size* ⇨L11GNⅥ

Ⅶ. *Keego*「敬語」〈2〉: regular honorifics

Examples

① A：木村先生はいらっしゃいますか。
Is Kimura-sensee in?

B：先生はお帰りになりました。
He has already gone home.

② A：けさの新聞、お読みになりましたか。
Did you read this morning's newspaper?

B：はい、読みました。
Yes, I did.

【*Explanation*】

1. Formation of regular honorifics

Recall the irregular honorific verbs we saw in Lesson 9: fortunately, there is a regular way of forming honorific verbs from most Group Ⅰ and Ⅱ verbs, as shown below:

GN

> お ＋ ［V (base)］＋ になる／なります

話す → お話しになる／お話しになります
帰る → お帰りになる／お帰りになります

1. 木村先生がお話しになります。
   Kimura-sensee will speak.

2. 林さんは何時ごろ家にお帰りになりますか。
   About what time will Hayashi-san return home?

Note that the honorific forms of some verbs, like the Group Ⅰ verbs 行く *to go* and 言う *to say,* Group Ⅱ verbs いる *to stay,* 見る *to see* and Group Ⅲ verbs 来る *to come* and する *to do,* cannot be formed using the pattern above; instead, the irregular honorific verbs introduced in Lesson 9 are used. ⇨L9GNⅥ

2. Honorific requests

You will hear very polite requests at department stores, banks, restaurants, or when you talk to a telephone operator.

お待ちください。	*Please wait.*
お話しください。	*Please speak.*
おかけください。	*Please sit down.*

These are much more polite than:

待ってください。
話してください。
かけてください。

The formation of such super polite requests is as follows.

（1）Group Ⅰ, Ⅱ verbs

$$\boxed{\text{お ＋ [V (base)] ＋ ください}}$$

とる → おとりください。 *Please take (one/some).*

1. お入りください。 *Please enter.*
   はい

2. 少々お待ちください。 *Please wait a moment.*
   しょうしょう　ま

There are again some exceptions which do not follow the regular formation:

見てください。 → ごらんください。 *Please take a look.*
み

寝てください。 → お休みください。 *Please go to bed/lie down.*
ね　　　　　　　　　やす

（2）Group Ⅲ verbs

する	ご／お ＋ verbal noun ＋ ください
来る く	おいでください

連絡する → ご連絡ください *Please contact me/us.*
れんらく

電話する → お電話ください *Please call me.*
でんわ

1. あしたもう一度お電話ください。 *Please call again tomorrow.*
   いちど

2. どうぞ、こちらにおいでください。 *Please come this way.*

Conversation Notes

<*General Information*>

1. Department stores in Japan

Department stores were previously called **百貨店（ひゃっかてん）** but now the term **デパート** has become popular. They are usually open from 10:00a.m. until 7:00p.m. every day with the exception of one day per week （**定休日，ていきゅうび**） when closed. The **定休日** differs from store to store.

a. Directory of a department store

Store directories indicating what is available on each floor are found at the entrance, as well as by the elevators and escalators. The major department stores also have handout copies of the directory available in English at the information counter.

The standard arrangement is as follows:

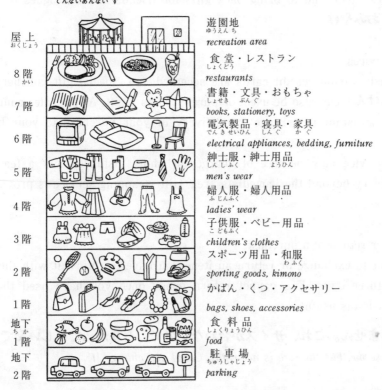

【店内案内図】 *Department store Directory*
てんないあんない ず

屋 上 おくじょう	遊園地 ゆうえんち recreation area
	食堂・レストラン しょくどう restaurants
8 階 かい	書籍・文具・おもちゃ しょせき ぶんぐ books, stationery, toys
7 階	電気製品・寝具・家具 でんきせいひん しんぐ かぐ electrical appliances, bedding, furniture
6 階	紳士服・紳士用品 しんしふく ようひん men's wear
5 階	婦人服・婦人用品 ふじんふく ladies' wear
4 階	子供服・ベビー用品 こどもふく children's clothes
3 階	スポーツ用品・和服 わふく sporting goods, kimono
2 階	かばん・くつ・アクセサリー bags, shoes, accessories
1 階	食料品 しょくりょうひん food
地下 ち か 1 階	駐車場 ちゅうしゃじょう parking
地下 2 階	

b. Sales

In a department store one cannot haggle for a cheaper price, but there are reductions in special sales called **セール** (*sale*), **バーゲン** (*bargain*) or **大売り出し** (**お おうりだし**, *big special*).

Other signs you will see include:

超特価	ちょうとっか	*super special price*
お買得品	おかいどくひん	*bargain goods*
半額	はんがく	*half price*
２０％引き	２０パーセントびき	*20% off*
２割引	２わりびき	*20% discount*

There are two big traditional gift-giving seasons in Japan. One is **お中元** (**おちゅ うげん**, *mid-summer gift*) in July, the other is **お歳暮** (**おせいぼ**, *end-of-year gift*) in December. Every department store puts on big sales during these two periods. Of course, gifts are given at other times, too, often for a specific purpose. **お祝い** (**おいわ い**) is a congratulatory gift, which may be given on auspicious occasions like weddings (although giving money is more common in this case), or the child of an acquaintance (often a senior colleague, or a personal friend) having passed an entrance examination. **お礼** (**おれい**), on the other hand, is a gift given in return for favours received.

The Japanese also tend to bring back gifts for friends and colleagues from trips; these are called **おみやげ**.

c. Various services

Besides cash, various credit cards are accepted, too. Special gift vouchers (**商品 券，しょうひんけん**) can also be used, or purchased as a gift. At the sales counter you can ask a shop assistant to arrange for delivery of your purchase to your home or elsewhere.

Delivery service may be free of charge for short distances, but a fee will be charged for delivery beyond the immediate area. Gift wrapping service is provided free of charge.

d. Exchange or return of a purchase

If you want to exchange or return an item, you have to return it with the receipt within two or three days. You cannot return goods once you have used them. The following expression is useful:

すみません。これ、サイズが合わないので、とりかえてほしいんですけど。
Excuse me, but the size is not right. Could you change it?

2. Expressions used in a department store

a. In the elevator

Many department stores still use specially trained girls to operate their elevators and announce floors, although some stores have replaced them with pre-recorded messages. In some stores no announcements are made and customers have to push the buttons themselves.

Here are some set phrases that you may hear in the elevator.

① ご来店 ┃ くださいまして ┃ 、ありがとうございます。
　　らいてん ┃ いただきまして ┃

Thank you very much for coming to our store.

② 上へ ┃ まいります。　　　　　　*Going up.*
　　うえ ┃
　　下へ ┃　　　　　　　　　　　　*Going down.*
　　した ┃

③ ご利用階数をお知らせください（ませ）。
　　りようかいすう　　　し
　　　　　　　　　　　　　　　Which floor, sir/madam?

④ かしこまりました。　　　　　　*Certainly, sir/madam.*

⑤ おあと、ございませんか。　　　*Any other floors?*

⑥ ドアが閉まります。　　　　　　*The door is going to close.*
　　　　　し

⑦ お待たせいたしました。　　　　*Sorry to have kept you waiting.*
　　　ま

⑧ 〜の売り場でございます。　　　*(This is) the floor for 〜.*
　　　　　う　ば

b. At the sales counter

When a customer first enters a store or section, an assistant will often say 「**いらっしゃいませ** (*welcome*)」 and ask 「**何かおさがしですか。** (*Are you looking for*
　　　　　　　　　　　　　　　　なに
something? = May I help you?)」. You can find out where to find something by using 「**〜**
はどこにありますか。 (*Where is 〜?*)」 or 「**〜、ありますか。** (*Do you have 〜?*)」.
When you are looking at something and an assistant asks 「**いかがですか。** (*How do you*
like it?)」, you can ask for advice using the expressions given under CN S-3 below, or
you can just say 「**いえ。ちょっと見ているだけですから。** (*No thank you. I'm just*
　　　　　　　　　　　　　　み
looking.)」.

You can try on clothes in a fitting room (**試着室，しちゃくしつ**). Remember that
shirts, underwear, socks and the like cannot normally be tried on.

c. Announcements

In a department store you may hear various announcements, from lost children and other people being paged to information about special events or entertainments. Below are some examples:

① お呼び出しを申し上げます。横浜からおこしの田中さま、横浜からおこしの田中さま、いらっしゃいましたら、1階の案内所までおこしください。

Calling Mr./Ms. Tanaka from Yokohama. Please come to the information counter on the 1st floor.

② ご来店くださいまして、まことにありがとうございます。本日は、6階、催し物場におきまして、九州うまいもの展を行っております。どうぞみなさま、おさそいあわせの上、ご来場くださいませ。

Thank you very much for coming to our store. Today we are having a "Kyushu Food Fair" at the special exhibition space on the 6th floor. Please come along with friends and family.

If you become separated from your companions in a department store, you can go to the information counter and ask for them to be paged.

d. Information on *Keego* expressions

Shop assistants use very polite expressions to customers. Although you will not normally reply in such polite language, you still need to be able to understand them.

<*Keego* expressions>		<Ordinary expressions>	
まいります	=	行きます／来ます	*to go, to come*
いたします	=	します	*to do*
おります	=	います	*to stay*
ございます	=	あります	*to exist, to have*
〜でございます	=	〜です	*to be*

You will find more information on such ***keego*** (humble) expressions in L18GN I.

3. Colours, patterns and sizes of clothes

a. Colours（**色，いろ**）⇨L14CN2

b. Patterns（**柄，がら**）

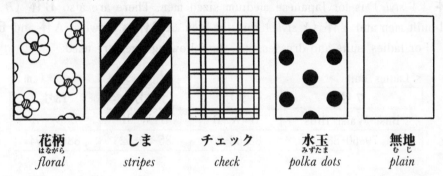

花柄 はながら *floral*	しま *stripes*	チェック *check*	水玉 みずたま *polka dots*	無地 む じ *plain*

c. Sizes（**サイズ**）

For sweaters, T-shirts and such like, the following sizes are used, although sizes vary according to the maker.

＜Men's shirts＞　　　　　　　　　　　　　　　　　　　　　　　　　　（cm）

Size	Chest	Shoulders	Sleeves	Length
L L ＝extra large	96~104	52	57	72
L ＝large	90~98	50	55	70
M ＝medium	84~92	48	53	68
S ＝small	78~86	46	51	66
F ＝free	M ～ L			

＜Ladies' blouses＞　　　　　　　　　　　　　　　　　　　　　　　　（cm）

Size	Bust	Shoulders	Sleeves	Length
L L ＝extra large	93~101	51	51	65
L ＝large	86~94	50	51	64
M ＝medium	79~87	48	50	62
S ＝small	72~80	46	49	60
F ＝free	M ～ L			

For men's suits, jackets, etc., the following sizes（**～号，ごう**）are used:

<Men's suits> 🕴 (cm)

	4号	**5号**	**6号**	**7号**
	Height-Chest-Waist	H – C – W	H – C – W	H – C – W
A体	165-90-73	170-92-77	175-94-81	180-96-85
AB体	165-94-77	170-96-81	175-98-85	180-100-89

A体（*A style*）is for Japanese medium sized men. There are also **B体**（*B style*）for well-built men and **Y体**（*Y style*）for slim men. **AB体** is between **A体** and **B体**.

For ladies' suits and dresses, etc., the following sizes are used:

<Ladies' suits> 👤 (cm)

7号	**9号**	**11号**	**13号**
Bust-Waist-Hips	B – W – H	B – W – H	B – W – H
79-60-88	82-63-90	85-66-92	88-69-94

Shoe size is indicated in centimeters in Japan. These sizes can be combined with "E", "EE" or "EEE" for feet with a wide fitting:

店員：サイズは何センチですか。
What/How many centimeters is your size?

客 ：ええと、24.5なんですけど。はばが広いの、ありますか。
Let me see... 24.5cm. Do you have that in a wide fitting?

店員：じゃ、こちらはいかがでしょう。24.5のEEです。
How about this one? It's 24.5 EE.

The biggest size in men's shoes you can usually find in Japanese department stores is 27cm or 27.5cm. For bigger sizes, you have to go to a shoe shop specializing in outsize shoes.

<Strategies>

S-1. How to find what you want

To find what you want, you need to give information about your size, favourite colour, design, etc. You will find some useful expressions below:

a. Colours, patterns and size（**色，柄，サイズ**）
いろ　がら

You can combine words indicating colour, pattern and size （⇨ CN3）in the following way:

> <Colour/size/design, etc.> の ［N］　｜　（が）ありますか。
> 　｜（が）ありませんか。
> 　｜（を）見せてください。
> み

① **すみません。赤と白のしまのワンピース、ありますか。**
　　　　 あか　しろ
Excuse me. Do you have a dress with red and white stripes?

② **こいピンクのくつで23.5の、ありませんか。**
Do you have a pair of 23.5cm dark pink shoes?

③ **あのうすい青の水玉のシャツ、みせてください。**
　　　　　　　　 あお　みずたま
Please show me that light blue shirt with the polka dots.

b. Design（**デザイン**）

> <part>が ［A］
> **大きい／小さい／長い／短い／ふとい／ほそい**
> 　おお　　ちい　　なが　　みじか
> *big　／small　／long　／short ／thick　／thin*

えり　*collar*
ボタン　*button*
そで　*sleeve*
ベルト　*belt*

c. When you want something in the same colour but in a different size, or in the same size but in a different colour, the following expressions can be used:

55

| この | 色
サイズ
形
デザイン | で ＜colour/pattern/size＞ の、 | ありますか。
ありませんか。
見せてください。 |

① **この色でMの、ありますか。**
Do you have an M size in this colour?

② **このサイズで青いの、ありますか。**
Do you have this size in blue?

③ **この形でもう少し大きいの、ありませんか。**
Do you have this design in a slightly bigger size?

④ **このデザインでちがう色の、ありませんか。**
Do you have this design in a different colour?

⑤ **この形で花柄の、見せてください。**
Please show me this design with a floral pattern.

S-2. How to ask for advice

a. To ask an assistant for advice, the following expressions are useful:

| ［N］は | ぼく 🚹　には ［A／NA］
私 | かな。🅖
かしら。🅖🚺
でしょうか。🄴 |

I wonder if ［N］ is too ［A/NA］ for me.

① **このLLっていうのは、ぼくには大きいかな。**
Is this LL (XL) size too big for me, I wonder?

② **この色、私にはちょっとじみかしら。🚺**
Is this colour perhaps too subdued for me?

③　これ、私には、はででしょうか。
Is this too loud for me?

b. To help you choose from several items, you can ask for advice, using the following comparative questions: ⇨GNⅢ

⇨GNⅢ

[N1] と [N2] と｜どちら｜が｜いい。↗ 😊
　　　　　　｜どっち😊｜　｜いいかな。😊
　　　　　　　　　　　　　　いいかしら。😊👤
　　　　　　　　　　　　　　いいでしょうか。🈁

Which is better, [N1] *or* [N2]*?*

＜group＞の中で どれが 一番｜いい。↗ 😊
　　　　　　　　　　　　　　いいかな。😊
　　　　　　　　　　　　　　いいかしら。👤😊
　　　　　　　　　　　　　　いいでしょうか。🈁

Which one is the best among ＜group＞?

①😊A：赤いのと青いのと、どっちがいいかな。
I wonder which is better, the red one or the blue one.

B：そうだなあ。青いほうがいいんじゃないか。↗ 👕
Let me see. I suppose the blue one is better.

②😊A：あの無地のスカートとこの花柄のとどっちがいいかしら。👤
I wonder which is better, that plain skirt or this skirt with the floral pattern.

B：ううん……。どっちもいいんじゃない。↗
Hmm... They are both nice.

③🈁A：あの３つの中でどれが一番いいでしょうか。
Which do you think is the best of those three?

B：そうですね。白いのが一番いいんじゃないでしょうか。
Let me see. I suppose the white one is the best.

cf. ～んじゃない／んじゃないか／んじゃないでしょうか are used to express one's opinion. ⇨L17CN1, L22GNⅣ

c. If you are looking for a present, you can ask a shop assistant for advice by describing the age, sex, taste, etc. of the person the present is intended for:

<person>に<occasion>のプレゼントをさがして(い)るん｜です｜けど、
　　　　　　　　　　　　　　　　　　　　　　　　だ

どんなのが いい｜でしょうか。📷
　　　　　　　｜かな。🅒
　　　　　　　｜かしら。↗🅒👤

I'm looking for a present for 〈person〉 for 〈occasion〉.
What do you think is suitable?

① 母に誕生日のプレゼントをさがしてるんですけど、どんなのがいいで
　　はは　たんじょう び
しょうか。50歳ぐらいなんですけど。📷
　　　　　さい
I'm looking for a birthday present for my mother. What sort of present would be nice, do you think? She's about 50 years old.

② 友だちに結婚のプレゼントをさがしてるんだけど、どんなのがいいか
　　とも　　けっこん
な。30ぐらいの男性なんだけど。🅒
　　　　　　　だんせい
I'm looking for a wedding present for my friend. What would be appropriate, I wonder. He's about 30 years old.

S-3. How to decline politely

When an assistant suggests something you don't like, you can express your disagreement with 「〜のほうがいいんですけど。」or 「ちょっと……。」in a puzzled manner.「ううん……。↘(*Hmm*)」,「そうですね。↘(*Let me see*)」and「でも。↘(*But*)」can also be used to decline politely.

① 店員：いかがでございますか。
　　てんいん

　　客：ううん……。↘ もうちょっと大きいほうがいいんですけど。
　　きゃく　　　　　　　　　　　　　　　　　おお
　　Hmm... I prefer a slightly bigger size.

② 店員：それじゃ、こちらなどは。

　　客：サイズはいいんですけど、デザインがちょっとね。
　　The size is O.K., but the design is a bit...

③　店員：こちらなど、最近流行のデザインですが。
てんいん　　　　　　　　　　　さいきんりゅうこう
　　This is a design which is in fashion at the moment.

　　客：そうねえ。↘　色がちょっと……。
　　きゃく　　　　　　　いろ
　　Let me see. The colour is a bit...

④　店員：とてもよくお似合いですよ。
　　　　　　　　　　　　に　あ
　　It suits you very well.

　　客：ううん……。↘　でも。↘
　　Hmm... . But... .

Recall that「～けど（*but*）……。」and「～が（*but*）……。」signal that the speaker wants the listener to continue the conversation. ⇨L5CN, L7GNⅢ, L8CN S-2

To end the conversation,「またにします。（*Some other time.*）」or「また来ますから。
（*I'll come again.*）」can be used. わるいけど or すみませんけど（*I'm sorry, but*）will add a degree of politeness to your refusal to buy.

①　店員：こちらなど、いかがですか。

　　客：ええと、もう少し明るい色のほうがいいんですけど。
　　　　　　　　　　すこ　あか　いろ
　　Let me see, I prefer one with a brighter colour.

　　店員：じゃ、こちらなどいかがでしょう。

　　客：そうねえ。↘　色はいいんですけど、形がちょっと。
　　　　　　　　　　　　　　　　　　　　かたち
　　Hmm. The colour is O.K., but the shape's a bit...

　　店員：それじゃ、こちらは。

　　客：あの、すみませんけど、また来ますから。

　　店員：そうですか。どうもありがとうございました。

②　店員：こちらは最近流行のデザインですが。

　　客：ううん……。↘　でもねえ。↘

　　店員：よくお似合いですよ。
　　It suits you very well.

　　客：ううん。↘　わるいけど、またに ｜ するよ。♂
　　　　　　　　　　　　　　　　　　　　　　　　　｜ するわ。♀

59

ちょっとおもしろい話

あなたの国では、一年に何日ぐらい休みますか。日本では、土曜日や日曜日のほかに、次のような国民の祝日（National Holidays）があります。

1月1日	元日	がんじつ	New Year's Day
1月15日	成人の日	せいじんのひ	Coming-of-Age Day
2月11日	建国記念の日	けんこくきねんのひ	National Foundation Day
3月20日	春分の日	しゅんぶんのひ	Vernal Equinox Day
4月29日	みどりの日	みどりのひ	Green Day
5月3日	憲法記念日	けんぽうきねんび	Constitution Day
5月5日	こどもの日	こどものひ	Children's Day
9月15日	敬老の日	けいろうのひ	Respect-for-the-Aged Day
9月23日	秋分の日	しゅうぶんのひ	Autumnal Equinox Day
10月10日	体育の日	たいいくのひ	Sports Day
11月3日	文化の日	ぶんかのひ	Culture Day
11月23日	勤労感謝の日	きんろうかんしゃのひ	Labour Thanksgiving Day
12月23日	天皇誕生日	てんのうたんじょうび	The Emperor's Birthday

祝日が日曜日と重なっているときは、その次の月曜日も休みになります。これを振替休日（substitute holiday）と言います。それから、正月はふつう1月1日から3日まで休みます。春分の日と秋分の日は、年によってかわります。

*重なる	to fall on
ふつう	usually, ordinarily
正月	the New Year
～によって	depending on ～

第11課

本屋で
ほんや
At a bookshop

OBJECTIVES:

GRAMMAR

Ⅰ. ～たら: *if/when* ～

Ⅱ. ～と思う: *think (that)* ～

Ⅲ. 《＋を verbs》 and 《－を verbs》: する verbs and
なる verbs〈3〉

Ⅳ. ～という～: ～ *called* ～

Ⅴ. で〈4〉: indicating an extent

Ⅵ. かかる for duration and cost

Ⅶ. に〈5〉: indicating frequency per unit

CONVERSATION

＜General Information＞
1. At a bookshop
2. Casual introductions

＜Strategies＞
S-1. How to ask for something to be done for you
—1.
S-2. How to order a book
S-3. How to cancel your order

61

Model Conversation

(1)

Characters : Tanaka(田中), Lisa Brown(リサ・ブラウン), Yamashita(山下), Anil Sharma(アニル・シャルマ), a shop assistant(店員)

Situation : Tanaka-san and Brown-san are in a bookshop, looking for a book. They meet Yamashita-san and Sharma-san, and introductions are made.

Flow-chart :

Meeting by chance	Inside the bookshop

↓

Introduction

―本屋の中で―

山 下　：あ、田中さん。

田 中　：あら。

　　　　　＊　　＊　　＊

山 下　：(To Tanaka-san) あ、紹介するよ。インドのアニルさん。

田 中　：こんにちは。

シャルマ：はじめまして。アニル・シャルマです。

山 下　：同じ研究室なんだ。

　　　　　(To Sharma-san) 田中さん。

田 中　：田中です。よろしく。

　　　　　(To Yamashita-san and Sharma-san) あ、こちら、リサ・ブラウンさん。

ブラウン：リサです。はじめまして。

田 中　：イギリスから来たの。

　　　　　(To Brown-san) 山下さん。

山 下　：よろしく。山下です。

シャルマ：よろしく。アニルって呼んでください。

ブラウン：アニルさん、専門は。

シャルマ：山下さんと同じ、コンピュータです。

ブラウン：そうですか。

（2）

Characters ：Tanaka(田中)，a shop assistant(店員)

Situation ：Tanaka-san is looking for a book entitled "Business Administration in Japanese Companies". She is told by the shop assistant that it is out of stock, so she places an order.

Flow-chart ：

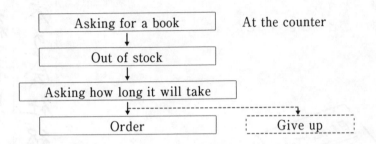

MC

―本屋のカウンターで―

田　中：すみません。

店　員：はい。

田　中：『日本の会社経営』という本が見つからないんですけど。

店　員：『日本の会社経営』ですね。

田　中：ええ。

店　員：少々お待ちください。

　　　　　・　　・　　・

店　員：申しわけありません。ただいま切らしておりますが。

　　　　＊　　　　＊　　　　＊

田　中：そうですか。

　　　　じゃ、注文したいんですけど、どのくらいかかりますか。

店　員：そうですね。2週間ほどで入ると思いますが。

田　中：そうですか。

　　　　＊　　　　＊　　　　＊

田　中：それじゃ、2冊お願いします。

店　員：はい。じゃ、こちらに書いてください。

田　中：はい。(Filling in the slip)

田　中：あのう出版社がわからないんですけど。

店　員：あっ、けっこうですよ。

田　中：はい。（Handing her the slip）これでいいですか。
店　員：はい。
　　　　じゃ、本が入りましたら、ご連絡します。
田　中：じゃ、お願いします。
　　　　　　・　・　・
店　員：あっ、これ、ひかえです。
田　中：あ、どうも。
店　員：ありがとうございました。

注 文 票		
題名	著者	出版社
日本の会社経営	大森和男	
定価	3,500円	
住所 TEL.	松見市さくら町 松見大学 1-1 学生宿舎 3-201 0298-53-2472	
氏名	田中みどり	

Report

　田中さんはよく本を読みます。一週間に2回ぐらい本屋へ行って、本をさがします。きのうもリサさんといっしょに『日本の会社経営』という本を買いに行きました。

　本が見つからなかったので、本屋の店員に聞きました。店員は、いま切らしているが、注文したら2週間ぐらいで入ると言いました。それで、注文票に本の題名と自分の住所、電話番号、氏名を書いて、注文しました。店員は本が入ったら連絡すると言いました。

New Words and Expressions

Words in the conversation

本屋	ほんや	bookshop
紹介する	しょうかい（する）	to introduce
同じ	おなじ	the same
カウンター		counter
会社	かいしゃ	company
経営	けいえい	management, business administration
見つかる	みつかる	to be found
ただいま		right now, at the moment
切らす	きらす	to be out of stock
どのくらい		how long ＝どのぐらい
かかる		(it) takes...
〜週間	〜しゅうかん	〜 week(s)
〜ほど		about 〜　＝〜ぐらい
入る	はいる	to come in, to enter
思う	おもう	to think
〜冊	〜さつ	counter for books
出版社	しゅっぱんしゃ	publishing company
連絡する	れんらく（する）	to contact
ひかえ		copy, duplicate

＜Expressions in the conversation＞

同じ研究室なんだ。　　　　　　　　　　　(He is) in the same section as I.
おな　けんきゅうしつ

　　〜と同じだ (the same as 〜) can be used as follows:

① リサさんは田中さんと同じ専門です。
　　　　　　たなか　　　　せんもん
Lisa's major is the same as Tanaka's.

② きょうの予定はきのうと同じです。
　　　　よてい
Today's schedule is the same as yesterday's.

③ その本は先生のと同じですか。
Is that book the same as the teacher's?

申しわけありません。 　　　　　　　　　　　　*We are very sorry.*

ただいま切らしておりますが。 　　　　　　　*It is out of stock now (, but what can I do for you?)*

　　　Use of **が** at the end of a sentence ⇨CN S-1

どのくらいかかりますか。 　　　　　　　　　*How long will it take?*

　　　かかる ⇨CN Ⅵ

2 週間ほどで入ると思いますが。 　　　　　*I think it will come in about two weeks (, but do you want to order?)* **〜が** ⇨CN S-1

　　　<thing>**が入る** means *An order comes in.*
　　　cf.<person>**が入る** means *to enter (a place).*

出版社がわからないんですけど。 　　　　　*I don't know the name of the publisher (, but what shall I do?)*

　　　〜けど。 ⇨L6CN S-5, 11CN S-1

けっこうですよ。 　　　　　　　　　　　　　*That's all right./It doesn't matter.*

　　　　　　　　　　　　　　　　　　　　　　　⇨まとめ3BⅡ1

本が入りましたら、ご連絡します。 　　　　*We'll contact you when the book comes in.*

　　　〜たら ⇨GN I

Words in the report

よく		*often*
〜回	〜かい	*time(s)*
さがす		*to look for, to search*
注文票	ちゅうもんひょう	*written order, order form*
題名	だいめい	*title* ＝書名（しょめい）
自分の	じぶんの	*her, his, one's*
住所	じゅうしょ	*address*
氏名	しめい	*full name* ＝名前（なまえ）

Grammar Notes

I. ～たら: *if/when~*

Examples

① ごはんを食べたら、出かけましょう。
When we've had (our) meal, let's go out.

② 暑かったら、まどを開けてもいいですよ。
If you are hot, you may open the window.

③ わからなかったら、辞書を見てください。
If/When you don't understand, look it up in the dictionary.

【*Explanation*】

The above sentences consist of {S₁} ＋たら, {S₂} . たら joins {S₁} and {S₂} with the implication that when {S₁} is realized, {S₂} will also be realized. The English equivalent of たら is *when* or *if*, or sometimes *after*.

As seen from the table below, the **-tara** form is made up by adding ら to the plain past (occasionally polite past) form of a verb, adjective, or [N]＋です.

⇨L5GN I / II / III , L6GN I , L8GN I / II

-tara form		Plain non-past	Plain past	-tara form
[V]	Pos.	wakaru	wakatta	wakattara
	Neg.	wakaranai	wakaranakatta	wakaranakattara
[A]	Pos.	takai	takakatta	takakattara
	Neg.	takaku nai	takaku nakatta	takaku nakattara

[NA] [N]	Pos.	genki da ame da	genki datta ame datta	genki dattara ame dattara
	Neg.	genki ja nai ame ja nai	genki ja nakatta ame ja nakatta	genki ja nakattara ame ja nakattara

1. Use of {S₁} ＋たら, {S₂}

1) {S₁} ＋たら indicates a condition for the occurrence of {S₂}. Note that {S₂} can express intention, request or obligation, etc., but not a factual statement in the present tense.

1. **あした雨が降ったら、行きません。**
   If it rains tomorrow, I will not go.

2. **安かったら、買います。**
   If it's cheap, I'll buy it.

3. **授業が終わったら、ちょっと来てください。**
   When/After the class is over, please come to see me.

4. **あしたデパートが休みだったら、どうしましょうか。**
   If the department store isn't open tomorrow, what shall we do?

2) When a たら sentence uses the past tense, the implication is that {S₂} came as a surprise or realization:

5. **山田さんに聞いたら、わかりました。**
   After asking Yamada-san, I understood.

6. **デパートで買物していたら、田中さんに会いました。**
   When I was shopping at the department store, I met Tanaka-san.

7. **宿舎に帰ったら、国から手紙が来ていました。**
   When I returned to the dormitory, a letter had come/I found a letter from home.

2. ＜question word＞＋〜たらいいですか: asking for suggestions

The combination ＜question word＞＋ -tara form can be used to ask for advice:

1. **A：あした何時に来たらいいですか。**
   What time shall I come tomorrow?

B：9時ごろ来てください。

じ　　き
Come around nine.

2. A：奨学金のことはどこで聞いたらいいでしょうか。

しょうがくきん　　　　　　　　　き
Where should I ask about scholarships?

B：事務所で聞いたらいいですよ。

じ　む　しょ　　き
You can ask at the office.

3. A：外国人登録証をなくしたんですが、どうしたらいいでしょうか。

がいこくじんとうろくしょう
I lost my alien registration card. What shall I do?

B：すぐ警察に届けてください。

けいさつ　とど
Report it to the police immediately.

Ⅱ. ～と思う: *think (that)* ～
おも

Examples

① 漢字はおもしろいと思います。　　　　*I think Kanji are interesting.*

かんじ

② A：この計画をどう思いますか。　　　*What do you think of this plan?*

けいかく

B：とてもいいと思います。　　　　　*I think it is very good.*

③ 新しい車を買いたいと思っています。　*I am thinking about buying a new car.*

あたら　　くるま　か

【*Explanation*】

{S [plain]} と 思う *think (that)* ～ can be used to express your own thoughts, feelings, opinions, ideas, guesses and intentions, etc., and ask about those of other people （②A）.

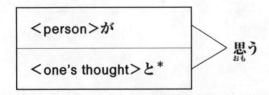

→ 私が＜漢字がおもしろい＞と思う。　*I think 〈Kanji are interesting〉.*

わたし

* The particle と indicates that the preceding sentence or words are a quotation.

⇨L9GNⅡ

私が is normally omitted (except for emphasis), because 〜と思う always refers to the speaker's thoughts.

Note that only plain forms are used before と思う:

1. ○ あした手紙が来ると思います。　　*I think the letter will come tomorrow.*

   × あした手紙が来ますと思います。

2. ○ きょう銀行は休みだと思いますか。　*Do you think the bank is closed today?*

   × きょう銀行は休みですと思いますか。

To express a thought or idea you have at the time/moment of your statement, {S [plain]} と思っている *am thinking* is used (③):

A：夏休みはどちらへ。
Where will you go in the summer holidays?

B：北海道に行きたいと思っています。
I'm thinking about going to Hokkaido.

Ⅲ. 《＋を verbs》 and 《－を verbs》：する verbs and なる verbs〈3〉

Examples

① 学生がドアを開けました。　　　*A student opened the door.*

② ドアが開いています。　　　　　*The door is open.*

③ A：その本はいつ入りますか。　　*When will the book come in?*

　 B：来週入ると思います。　　　　*I think it'll come in next week.*

【Explanation】

We saw before that する *to do* focuses on intentional action, while なる *to become* is concerned with the result of an action or happening. ⇨L3GNⅢ，L9GNⅤ

Japanese verbs can be divided into **する** and **なる** type verbs depending on whether the subject or actor controls the action or not. **する** verbs like 食べる *to eat*, 行く *to go*, 開ける *to open*, つける *to turn on* express intentional action, or an action that the actor can control. In contrast, **なる** verbs like 困る *to be in trouble*, わかる *to understand*, 開く *to open (by itself)*, つく *to come on* focus on the result of an action or happening and cannot be controlled by the subject. The two types are contrasted in the example below:

（１）私はドアを開ける。　　　　　（２）ドアが開く。
I open the door.　　　　　　　　　　*The door opens.*

 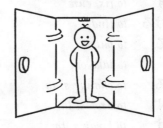

In (1), the subject 私 controls the opening of the door, whereas in (2) the opening of the door is the result of someone else's action which cannot be controlled by the subject ドア. Many verbs have two related forms, of which one is a **する** type, the other a **なる** type verb.

Now, many **する** verbs can take an object marked with **を**. Let's call these verbs 《＋を verbs》, and verbs which don't take **を**, 《－を verbs》. 《＋を verbs》 and 《－を verbs》 take the following structures, respectively.

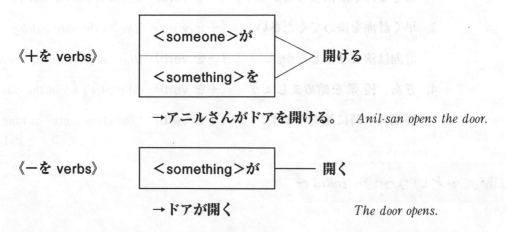

The following table lists some verbs that have corresponding pairs of 《＋を verbs》 and 《－を verbs》.

《＋を verbs》 transitive		《－を verbs》 intransitive (automatic) が	
開ける	to open something	開く	to be opened, open
閉める	to close s. th.	閉まる	to be closed, close
止める	to stop s. th.	止まる	to stop
決める	to decide　けいかく-plan	決まる	to be decided
つける	to turn on	つく	to come on
消す	to turn off	消える	to go out
始める	to begin s. th.	始まる	to begin
なおす	to fix, cure	なおる	to be fixed, be cured
見つける	to find	見つかる	to be found
入れる	to put in	入る	to come/go in
出す	to take out	出る	to come out
かえる	to change s. th.	かわる	to change
落とす	to drop s. th.　さいふ-wallet	落ちる	to drop, fall
こわす	to break s. th.	こわれる	to break, be broken
届ける	to deliver	届く	to be delivered

らんぼう-violent

1. ドアを閉めてもいいですか。　《＋を verb》　*May I close the door?*

   ドアが閉まります。　《－を verb》　*The door will close.*

2. 車を止めてください。　《＋を verb》　*Stop the car, please.*

   あそこに車が止まっています。《－を verb》　*A car is parked over there.*

3. 早く計画を決めてください。　《＋を verb》　*Decide the plan quickly.*

   計画は決まりましたか。　《－を verb》　*Has the plan been decided?*

4. さあ、授業を始めましょう。　《＋を verb》　*Well, let's begin the class.*

   授業は９時に始まります。　《－を verb》　*The class begins at nine.*

⇨まとめ4AⅢ

Ⅳ. ～という～: ~ called ~

Like [N] **というのは** (⇨L10GNV), [N₁] **という** [N₂], *[N₂] called [N₁]* is also used to refer to a thing or person that is unfamiliar to the listener and/or the speaker:

1. A：きのうルナという店に行きました。
   I went to a shop called Runa yesterday.

   B：そうですか。どんな店ですか。
   Really? What kind of shop is it?

2. さっき横山（さん）という人から電話が
   ありましたよ。
   There was a call from a person called
   Yokoyama a while ago.

V. 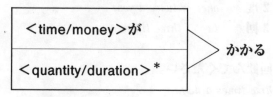 で〈4〉: indicating an extent

Preceded by a quantity, time or amount of money, で indicates an extent:

1. 3日でレポートを書きました。　　*I wrote a report in three days.*
2. 本は2週間で入ります。　　*The book will come in two weeks.*
3. このシャツを千円で買いました。　*I bought this shirt for 1000 yen.*
4. そのりんごはみっつで５００円です。*These apples are 3 for 500 yen.*

⇨L5GNⅦ

VI. かかる for duration and cost

かかる *it takes, it costs* takes the following structure.

| ＜time/money＞が |
| ＜quantity/duration＞* |

＞ かかる

→ （時間が）3日かかる。　　　　*It takes three days.*

→ （お金が）千円かかる。　　　　*It costs 1000 yen.*

* Recall that no structure particle is attached to counters（⇨L2GNⅥ）.

To ask about duration or cost, use **どのくらい** or **どのぐらい**（*how long, how much* or *how far*）.

A：東京から北海道まで飛行機でどのくらいかかりますか。
How long does it take from Tokyo to Hokkaido by plane?

B：1時間ぐらいかかります。　　*It takes about one hour.*

A：お金はどのぐらいかかりますか。*How much does it cost?*

B：1万5千円ぐらいだと思います。*I think it costs about 15000 yen.*

ぐらい／くらい can be attached after the quantity to indicate the approximate quantity.（⇨ まとめ3 A I for a list of units of time）

ごろ indicates the approximate **point** of time, therefore you cannot use ごろ for the approximate **duration** of time. ⇨L7GNV

○　きのう3時間ぐらい勉強しました。
I studied for about three hours yesterday.

×　きのう3時間ごろ勉強しました。

VII. 〈にく5〉: indicating frequency per unit

1日 日 }	に　3度	*three times a day*
1週間 週 }	に　2日	*two days a week*
1か月 月 }	に　{ 1回 3回 }	*once a month* *three times a month*
1年 年 }	に　{ 1、2度 2、3回 }	*once or twice a year* *two or three times a year*

1. この薬は1日に3回飲んでください。
Take this medicine three times a day.

2. 1週間に1回せんたくします。　　*I do the washing once a week.*

3. A：毎日学校に行きますか。　　*Do you go to school every day?*

　B：いえ、週に3日学校に行きます。*No, I go to school three days a week.*

⇨まとめ3A I

74

Conversation Notes

＜*General Information*＞

1. At a bookshop

a. Classification of books

In a bookshop, books are classified according to their subject matter. To locate a book, therefore, you have to look at the fields of study (⇨ L1NW) marked on the shelves as illustrated below:

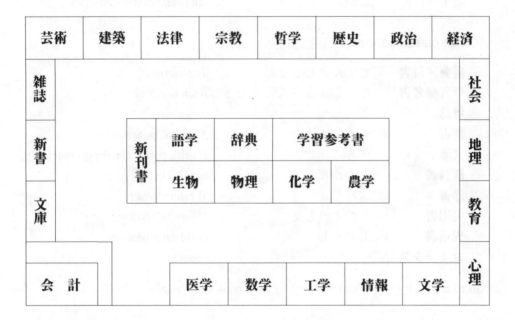

[Classification of books]

芸術	げいじゅつ	*art*
建築	けんちく	*architecture*
法律	ほうりつ	*law*
宗教	しゅうきょう	*religion*
哲学	てつがく	*philosophy*
歴史	れきし	*history*
政治	せいじ	*politics*
経済	けいざい	*economics*
社会	しゃかい	*society, sociology*

地理	ちり	geography
教育	きょういく	education
心理	しんり	psychology
文学	ぶんがく	literature
情報	じょうほう	information (science)
工学	こうがく	engineering
数学	すうがく	mathematics
医学	いがく	medical science
生物	せいぶつ	biology
物理	ぶつり	physics
化学	かがく	chemistry
農学	のうがく	agriculture
語学	ごがく	language and linguistics

[Other classifications]

辞典／辞書	じてん／じしょ	dictionaries
学習参考書	がくしゅうさんこうしょ	reference books
雑誌	ざっし	magazines
新書	しんしょ	Shinsho, paperbacks
文庫	ぶんこ	Bunko, pocket-sized paperbacks
新刊書	しんかんしょ	new books
洋書	ようしょ	Western books
実用書	じつようしょ	"How To" books
児童書	じどうしょ	children's books
コミックス		comics

Go to a nearby bookshop and try to find books in the above fields.

b. Information about a book

Information on a book, such as **書名(しょめい)** or **題名(だいめい)** for its title, **出版社(しゅっぱんしゃ)** or **発行所(はっこうじょ)** for publisher, **著者(ちょしゃ)** for author, **発行年(はっこうねん)** for year of publication, etc. can be found on the last page of a book. That page is called **おくづけ** (publisher's imprint).

The form called **注文票(ちゅうもんひょう)** or sometimes **予約票(よやくひょう)** requires you to fill in information on the book; compare the following examples of the **おくづけ** of a book and an order form for it:

＜おくづけ＞

SITUATIONAL FUNCTIONAL JAPANESE
VOLUME ONE: NOTES

1991年12月16日　　初版第 1 刷発行

著　者　　筑波ランゲージグループ
発行所　　株式会社　凡 人 社
　　　　　〒102 東京都千代田区麹町 6 － 2
　　　　　　　麹町ニュー弥彦ビル 2 F　電話 03－3472－2240
印刷所　　株式会社　イ セ ブ
　　　　　〒305 茨城県つくば市天久保 2 －11－20
　　　　　　　電話 0298－51－2515

You also have to write your name, address and telephone number on the form, enabling the shop assistant to inform you by mail or telephone of the book's arrival, usually after about one or two weeks. You keep a copy (**ひかえ**).

注　文　票		
書名	著者	発行所
SITUATIONAL FUNCTIONAL JAPANESE Vol.1 Notes	筑波ランゲージグループ	（株）凡人社
		¥3000
住所	松見市さくら町H 松見大学 学生宿舎 3-201	
氏名	田中みどり	
電話	（53）2472	

CN

2. Casual Introductions

In L1 you learned how to introduce yourself in a formal situation (⇨L1CN1, S-2); compare this with the casual introduction below:

Casual introduction   Formal introduction

In casual conversation complete sentences are not required, but adequate speed and fluency are necessary.

When introducing someone you know quite well, you can add some more information besides the name and nationality:

① 山下：あ、紹介するよ。　　　　　*Let me introduce (him to you).*

　　インドのアニルさん。　　　　*(This is) Anil from India.*

　　同じ研究室なんだ。　　　　　*(He is in) the same section as I.*

② 田中：リサ・ブラウンさん。　　　*(This is) Lisa Brown.*

　　イギリスから来たの。　　　　*(She)'s from England.*

78

<Strategies>

S-1. How to ask for something to be done for you —1.

Introduce such a request with **すみません** or **お願いします** (⇨L2CN S-2), or more politely, **ちょっとうかがいますが** or **ちょっとおたずねしたいんですが** (⇨L7CN S-3).

To ask for something, you can use one of the following:

~ （を） ｜ **ください。**　　　⇨L2CN S-2
　　　　　 お願いします。

~ （は） ｜ **ありますか。**　　　⇨L3CN S-1
　　　　　 ありませんか。

To ask someone to do something for you, you can, of course, use an expression of request like **[V-te] ください（ませんか）**.⇨L5GNⅣ; the Japanese, however, often prefer to use indirect ways of asking:

~ ｜ （が）**見つからないんですけど。**　　*I can't find* ~
　　 （を）**さがしているんですけど。**　　*I'm looking for* ~

① **『～』という本が見つからないんですけど。**
　 I can't find the book "～", but... (can you help me?)

② **『～』っていう本をさがして（い）るんですけど。**
　 I'm looking for a book called "～", but... (where can I find it?)

Used at the end of a sentence, **けど** or **が** is a more polite way of asking than **から** or **ので** because it implies hesitation to ask for something outright, leaving it to the listener to offer help. ⇨L10CN S-3　In a shop, you can ask 「**～が見つからないので、さがしてください。**(*I can't find* ～ *so please help*)」, but you must avoid making a request with **から** or **ので** to a senior.

79

S-2. How to order a book

a. Ordering a book

When the book you want is out of stock, you can order it. You have to fill in a written order and say as follows:

客：あの、注文、お願いします。
I'd like to place an order.

店員：はい。それじゃ、こちらにお願いします。
I see. Please (fill) in this (form), then.

b. Asking how long it takes   ⇨L2 S-3

どのくらいかかりますか can be used to ask how long it will take; the shop assistant might use the following to answer your question:

〈period〉ぐらい／ほど [V]（か）と思います。

Various expressions can be used to indicate that the speaker is unsure of the exact amount of time: 〈period〉＋**ちょっと** can be used to show that it is a little over the period indicated, whereas 〈period〉＋**ぐらい／くらい** and 〈period〉＋**ほど** express an approximate period: ⇨GNⅥ

① 客：あの、どのくらいかかりますか。

　店員：そうですね。2週間ちょっとかかるかと思いますが。
　Let me see; it'll take a little over 2 weeks.

② 客：ええと、どのくらいで来ますか。

　店員：そうですね。1週間ぐらいで入ると思いますけど。
　Let's see; it should come in about a week.

③ 客：どのくらいかかるでしょうか。

　店員：そうですね。3週間ほどだと思いますけど。
　Let's see; it should take about 3 weeks.

Other useful expressions are 〈period〉＋**以上**（*over* ～）and 〈period〉＋**以内**（*within* ～）. You may also hear「〈period〉＋**は かからないと思います**。（*It should take less than* ～.）」

c. Declining

If you don't want to place an order, you can say:

① 客_{きゃく}：ええと、どのくらいかかりますか。

　　店員_{てんいん}：そうですね。1か月以上_{げついじょう}かかると思_{おも}いますが。

　　客：1か月ですか。

　　店員：ええ。

　　客：あの、それじゃ、けっこうです。
　　　　Um, in that case it's all right.

② 客：これ、いくらですか。

　　店員：8500円_{えん}です。

　　客：85000円。
　　　　すみません。それじゃ、けっこうです。
　　　　Sorry, but I don't want it.

S-3. How to cancel your order

If you want to cancel your order, you should inform the bookshop as soon as possible. Money is not normally charged for cancelling a book order, but if you cancel some other kinds of reservation (e.g. hotel, tour ticket) or place an advance order, cancellation charges are sometimes incurred.

The following are example dialogues for the cancellation of a book. Instead of 取_とり けす (*to cancel*) you can also use the verb キャンセルする (*to cancel*).

① 客：あの、すみません。

　　店員：はい。

　　客：きのう『日本_{にほん}の会社経営_{かいしゃけいえい}』っていう本_{ほん}を注文_{ちゅうもん}したんですけど。
　　　　Yesterday I ordered the book "Business Administration in Japanese Companies", but...

　　店員：はい。（Looking for the order form）こちらですね。

　　客：あの、悪_{わる}いんですけど、これ、取_とりけしたいんですが。
　　　　Well, I'm sorry, but I'd like to cancel this order.

　　店員：あ、そうですか。わかりました。

CN

81

② 客：もしもし。○○書店ですか。

店員：はい。

　客：田中と申しますが、きのう注文した本のことなんですけど。
　　　My name is Tanaka, I ordered a book yesterday, but...

店員：はい。ええと、田中さま。（Looking for the order form）

　客：『経営学入門』っていう本なんですが。
　　　It's a book called "An Introduction to Business Administration".

店員：はい。『経営学入門』ですね。

　　　I see. "An Introduction to Business Administration"

　客：実は、ほかのところで見つけたんで、注文、取りけしたいんですけど。
　　　In fact, I found that book somewhere else, so I'd like to cancel my order.

店員：ああ、そうですか。キャンセルですね。わかりました。

　客：どうもすみません。

店員：いいえ。また、よろしくお願いします。

道を聞く
みち　き
Asking the way

OBJECTIVES:

GRAMMAR

Ⅰ. ～と（と〈4〉）: *if/when/whenever* ～
Ⅱ. ～ほうがいい: *giving advice*
Ⅲ. ～てから（から〈3〉）: *after* ～
Ⅳ. あと: *after*
Ⅴ. まえ: *before*
Ⅵ. を〈2〉: *marking the route*
Ⅶ. 見える and 聞こえる：する verbs and
　　み　　　き　　　　　　　なる verbs〈4〉
Ⅷ. ところ〈1〉: *place, at/by*（place）
Ⅸ. 〈quantity/duration〉＋は: *at least*
Ⅹ. ～め: *making ordinal numbers*

CONVERSATION

＜General Information＞

1. Location and landmarks

＜Strategies＞

S-1. How to ask for directions
S-2. How to give directions
S-3. How to go by public transport
S-4. How to confirm information －2.

Model Conversation

(1)

Characters ：Yamashita(山下)，passer-by A（通行人Ａ，female）

Situation ：Yamashita-san has been to the cinema. On his way home, he wants to buy a new video camera. He knows the name of the camera shop, but he does not know the way to the shop, so he asks a female passer-by how to get there.

Flow-chart ：

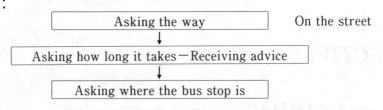

```
          ┌──────────────────────────────┐
          │       Asking the way         │        On the street
          └──────────────────────────────┘
                         ↓
    ┌──────────────────────────────────────────┐
    │ Asking how long it takes─Receiving advice │
    └──────────────────────────────────────────┘
                         ↓
        ┌──────────────────────────────────┐
        │   Asking where the bus stop is   │
        └──────────────────────────────────┘
```

―道で―

山　下　：あのう、すみません。

通行人Ａ：はい。

山　下　：安井カメラへ行きたいんですけど。

通行人Ａ：安井カメラ。

山　下　：ええ。

通行人Ａ：歩いて行くんですか。

山　下　：はい。

通行人Ａ：かなり遠いですよ。

山　下　：あ、そうですか。どのくらいかかりますか。

通行人Ａ：そうね。20分は、かかると思いますけど。

山　下　：20分ですか。

通行人Ａ：ええ。バスで行ったほうがいいんじゃないかしら。

山　下　：じゃ、そうします。

　　　　　　　　＊　　　　＊　　　　＊

山　下　：あの、バス停は。

通行人Ａ：ええと、ここをまっすぐ行くとね、

山　下　：はい。

84

通行人Ａ：あの、すぐ左にバス停がありますから、
山　下　：はい。
通行人Ａ：で、大森行きに乗って、２つ目ですよ。
山　下　：２つ目ですね。
通行人Ａ：ええ。あとは、降りてからまた聞いたほうがいいですよ。
山　下　：はい。ありがとうございました。
通行人Ａ：いいえ。

（２）

Characters ：Yamashita(山下), passer-by B（通行人Ｂ, male）

Situation ：Yamashita-san gets off the bus and asks a male passer-by how to get to the camera shop.

Flow-chart ：

```
┌─────────────────────────────────────────┐
│  Asking where the camera shop is         │
└─────────────────────────────────────────┘
                    ↓
┌─────────────────────────────────────────┐
│  Confirming the information              │
└─────────────────────────────────────────┘
```

―バスを降りたところで―

山　下　：すみません。
通行人Ｂ：はい。
山　下　：あの、安井カメラは、どこでしょうか。
通行人Ｂ：安井カメラね。
山　下　：ええ。
通行人Ｂ：あそこに、大きい道があるでしょう。
山　下　：ええ。
通行人Ｂ：あそこを右に曲がって５０メートルぐらい行くと、歩道橋があるから、
山　下　：右に５０メートルですね。
通行人Ｂ：そうそう。で、それを渡ると、右側にありますよ。
山　下　：歩道橋を渡って、右側。
通行人Ｂ：ええ。歩道橋のところから大きいかんばんが見えますから。
山　下　：ああ、わかりました。どうも。
通行人Ｂ：いいえ。

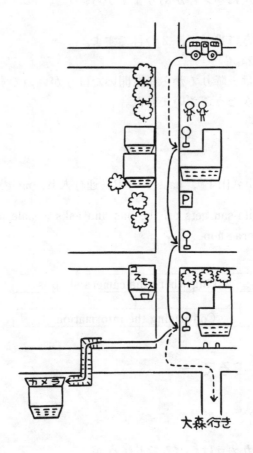

大森行き

Report

＜山下さんの日記＞
　映画を見たあとで、カメラ屋へ行った。その店は安くて有名だ。行き方を知らなかったので、女の人に道を聞いた。映画館の近くのバス停で大森行きのバスに乗って、二つ目で降りた。バスを降りてから、少し歩くとすぐ大きい通りがあった。そこを右に曲がって50メートルぐらい行くと、歩道橋があった。歩道橋のところからカメラ屋の大きいかんばんが見えたので、すぐわかった。ビデオカメラを買いたかったが、高かったので買わなかった。

New Words and Expressions

Words in the conversation

道	みち	*road*
通行人	つうこうにん	*passer-by*
安井カメラ	やすいカメラ	*Yasui Camera shop*
かなり		*fairly*
遠い	とおい	*far*
バス		*bus*
バス停	バスてい	*bus stop*
まっすぐ		*straight on*
大森	おおもり	*place name*
～行き	～いき／ゆき	*destination*
2つ目	ふたつめ	*the second*
降りる	おりる	*to get off*
あと		*the rest*
ところ		*place*
曲がる	まがる	*to turn*
メートル		*meter*
歩道橋	ほどうきょう	*footbridge*
渡る	わたる	*to cross*
右側	みぎがわ	*the right side*
かんばん		*signboard*
見える	みえる	*to be seen, to be visible*

MC

<Expressions in the conversation>

安井カメラに行きたいんですけど。　　　　*How do I get to Yasui Camera?*

バスで行ったほうがいいんじゃないかしら。*I think it might be better if you go by bus.*
⇨GNⅡ

　　　～たほうがいい recommends a course of action. **じゃないかしら** *I wonder if it isn't* is an indirect (i.e. polite) way of expressing one's opinion. The male equivalent of the female **かしら** is **かな**.

そうします。　　　　　　　　　　　　　　*I'll do that.*

　　そう refers to what the passer-by told Yamashita-san「バスで行ったほうが
いい。」; this need not be repeated as it is understood.

あとは、降りてからまた聞いたほうが　　　　*For the rest, you'd better ask someone after*
いいですよ。　　　　　　　　　　　　　　*getting off.*

　　あと is used as follows:

①　話のあとを聞きたい。
　　Tell me the rest of the story.

②　緑町 3 丁目までバスで行き、あとは歩いた。
　　I went by bus to Midoricho 3-choome and walked the rest (of the way).

で、大森行きに乗って、2つ目ですよ。　　　*Then, take the bus for Omori and get off at*
　　　　　　　　　　　　　　　　　　　　the 2nd stop.

　　〜目 is a counter indicating order. ⇨GN X

①　「大学正門」はここから 3 つ目です。
　　Daigakuseimon is the third one/stop from here.

②　下から 3 行目を見てください。
　　Look at the third line from the bottom.

③　左から 3 人目の人が田中さんです。
　　The third person from the left is Miss Tanaka.

あそこに大きい道があるでしょう。↗　　　　*You can see a wide road over there, can't*
　　　　　　　　　　　　　　　　　　　　you?

そうそう。　　　　　　　　　　　　　　　*ah hmm*

　　positive answer: そうです／はい

歩道橋のところから大きいかんばんが　　　　*You can see a big signboard from the*
みえますから。　　　　　　　　　　　　　*footbridge.*

　　ところ ⇨GN Ⅷ

Words in the report

映画	えいが	*film, cinema*
カメラ屋	カメラや	*camera shop*
有名（な）	ゆうめい（な）	*famous*
行き方	いきかた	*way of getting to a place*
映画館	えいがかん	*cinema*
すぐ		*soon*
通り	とおり	*street*
ビデオカメラ		*video camera*

MC

Grammar Notes

I. ⊛ ～と（とく4〉）: *if/when/whenever* ～

Examples

① 50メートル行くと、カメラ屋があります。
If you go 50 meters (down the street), there is a camera shop.

② 右に曲がると、駅が見えます。
When you turn right, you can see the station.

③ 漢字がわからないと、困りますよ。
If you don't know Kanji, you'll be in trouble.

④ 学生だと、安くなります。
For students, it's cheaper. (lit. If you're a student, it gets cheaper.)

【*Explanation*】

Recall the structure we saw in Lesson 11, {S₁}＋たら, {S₂}, as in

　　　雨が降ったら、行きません。　　　*If it rains, I won't go.*

{S₁ [plain non-past]} と, {S₂} is very similar in meaning to the structure with たら; here the implication is that {S₂} is always realized when {S₁} is realized.

Note that と, which is equivalent to *whenever, when* or *if* in English, can be preceded only by the plain non-past form of verbs, adjectives, and [N]＋です.

[V]	わかる わからない	
[A]	むずかしい むずかしくない	と、～
[NA]	元気だ 元気じゃない	
[N]	学生だ 学生じゃない	

90

1. Use of {S₁ [plain non-past]} ＋と, {S₂}

In a と sentence, the event described in {S₂} occurs as a natural consequence of that of {S₁}. と sentences are normally used for facts or habitual events.

1. まっすぐ行くと、駅があります。
   If you go straight on, you'll find the station.

2. このボタンを押すと、ランプがつきます。
   When you press this button, the lamp will come on.

3. ２月になると、このへんは雪が降ります。
   In February, it snows around here.
   (lit. When it becomes February, it snows around here.)

2. The difference between たら and と   ⇨L11GN I

1) Unlike with たら, {S₂} of a と sentence normally cannot express the speaker's intention, wish, request or suggestion:

1. ○　田中さんが来たら、始めましょう。
   When Tanaka-san comes, let's start.

   ×　田中さんが来ると、始めましょう。

2. ○　わからなかったら、聞いてください。
   If you don't understand, please ask.

   ×　わからないと、聞いてください。

2) The sequence of the two events connected by と is inevitable or habitual, whereas with たら the sequence is temporal or accidental. Therefore you should use と rather than たら to explain the steps of an experiment in a laboratory, for instance.

3) たら is more conversational than と, and is rarely used in written materials such as reports or theses.

3. Use of が and は in と sentences

1) When the subjects of {S₁} and {S₂} are different, either (1) or (2) can be used:

(1) リサさんがオーバーをぬぐと、アニルさんが／はハンガーにかけます。
   When Lisa-san takes off her coat, Anil-san puts it on a coat hanger.

(2) <u>アニルさんは</u>、<u>リサさんが</u>オーバーをぬぐと、ハンガーにかけます。

As for <u>Anil-san</u>, when <u>Lisa-san</u> takes off her coat, <u>he</u> puts it on a coat hanger.

As seen from the above examples, the subject of 〔S₁〕 (Lisa) can be marked by が only, whereas the subject of the 〔S₂〕 (Anil) can be marked by が or は when it is part of 〔S₂〕, or は only if it precedes 〔S₂〕 as a topic. The rule that the subject of 〔S₁〕 (a subordinate clause) is marked by が applies to other structures, too, including ～たら (⇨L11GN I), ～てから (⇨GN Ⅲ), ～とき (⇨L20GN Ⅳ), ～あとで (⇨GN Ⅳ), ～まえに (⇨GN V), etc.

2) When the subject of 〔S₁〕 and 〔S₂〕 is the same, it is mentioned only in 〔S₁〕, marked by は:

(3) <u>アニルさんは</u>、オーバーをぬぐと、ハンガーにかけます。

When <u>Anil-san</u> takes off his coat, <u>he</u> puts it on a coat hanger.

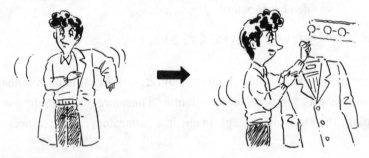

Ⅱ. ～ほうがいい: giving advice

Examples

① バスで行ったほうがいいですよ。
You'd better go by bus.

② 鈴木さんに聞いたほうがいいと思います。
I think you'd better ask Suzuki-san.

③　授業は休まないほうがいいです。
じゅぎょう　やす
You'd better not miss the class.

【*Explanation*】

Attached to the plain past positive or plain non-past negative of a verb, **ほうがいい** serves to make a suggestion or give advice.

[V-ta]	ほうがいい（です）	*had better....*
[V-nai]	ほうがいい（です）	*had better not....*

1.　薬を飲んだほうがいいです。　　*(You)'d better take some medicine.*
　　くすり　の

2.　薬は飲まないほうがいいです。　　*(You)'d better not take any medicine.*

ほうがいい is attached to the plain past positive, but the advice given pertains to the present/future. The plain non-past positive is also used at times, with the same meaning:

3.　日本語を話すほうがいいですよ。　*You'd better speak in Japanese.*
　　にほんご　はな

Ⅲ.　〜てから　（から〈3〉）: *after ～*

Examples

①　授業が終わってから、本屋に行きます。
　　　　お　　　　　　ほんや　い
I'll go to the bookshop after class is over.

②　先生に相談してから、決めたほうがいいですよ。
　　せんせい　そうだん　　　　き
You'd better decide after talking it over with your teacher.

【*Explanation*】

から attached to the **-te** form of a verb means *after doing*. As with other uses of the **-te** form, the final verb decides whether the sentence as a whole is non-past or past:

1. うちに帰ってから、何をしますか。
   What will you do after returning home?

2. うちに帰ってから、何をしましたか。
   What did you do after returning home?

Ⅳ. あと: *after*

あと *later, after* is a noun grammatically; it is used as follows:

1. [N] のあとで、{S}

1. 授業のあとでサッカーをしましょう。
   Let's play soccer after class.

2. 鈴木さんは仕事のあとで、ビールを飲みます。
   Suzuki-san drinks beer after work.

2. {S₁ [V-ta]} あとで、{S₂}

1. 昼ごはんを食べたあとで、本屋へ行きました。
   I went to the bookshop after I had lunch.

Again, the final verb decides whether the sentence as a whole is non-past or past:

2. こんばん勉強したあとで、何をしますか。
   What will you do after you study this evening?

3. ゆうべ勉強したあとで、何をしましたか。
   What did you do after you studied last night?

The meaning of {S₁ [V-ta]} あとで、{S₂} and {S₁ [V-te]} から、{S₂} is almost identical, the difference being that the former structure emphasizes that {S₂} takes place after the action of {S₁} has been COMPLETED, whereas in the latter {S₂} simply follows {S₁}. It is for this reason that あとで is attached to [V-ta].

V. まえ: *before*

まえ *before* is used as follows:

1. [N] のまえに、{S}

1. この薬は食事のまえに飲んでください。
Take this medicine before meals.

2. アニルさんは仕事のまえにジョギングをします。
Anil-san goes jogging before work.

2. {S₁ [V-(r)u]} まえに、{S₂}

1. 毎晩、寝るまえに手紙を書きます。
I write a letter every night before I go to bed.

2. A:日本へ来るまえに、日本語を勉強しましたか。
Did you study Japanese before you came to Japan?

B:いいえ、しませんでした。
No, I didn't.

Again, the final verb decides whether the whole sentence is non-past or past:

3. 毎晩、寝るまえに、おいのりをします。
I pray every night before I go to sleep.

4. ゆうべ、寝るまえに、おいのりをしました。
I prayed before I went to sleep last night.

Note that **まえ** is preceded by [V-(r)u] , indicating that the action of {S₁} is not yet completed when {S₂} is realized.

The same rules as explained in GN I 3 for と apply to the use of は and が with ～まえに and other structures such as ～てから:

5. アニルさんはうちへ帰ってから（帰ったあとで）、手紙を書きます。
Anil-san will write a letter after he returns home.

アニルさんは　リサさんが帰ってから（帰ったあとで）、手紙を書きます。
Anil-san will write a letter after Lisa-san returns home.

6. 田中さんは研究室に行くまえに、電話をしました。
   Tanaka-san telephoned before she went to the seminar room.

田中さんは　リサさんが研究室に行くまえに、電話をしました。
Tanaka-san telephoned before Lisa-san went to the seminar room.

Ⅵ. 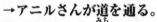 を〈2〉: marking the route

1. を: marking the route

通る *to pass* and 曲がる *to turn* take a structure where が marks the subject and
を the route which the movement follows:

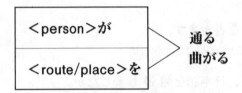

→アニルさんが道を通る。
Anil-san passes along the street.

→アニルさんがかどを曲がる。
Anil-san turns the corner.

Other verbs taking this structure include:

わたる	*to cross over*
歩く	*to walk*
走る	*to run*

→アニルさんが道をわたる。
Anil-san crosses the street.

→アニルさんが道を歩く。
Anil-san walks along the street.

2. Verbs taking を to mark the place from which one leaves

The verbs 出る _で *to go/come out, to leave* and おりる *to get off, to disembark* take を to mark the place from which one gets off or leaves:

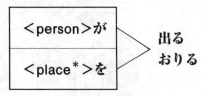

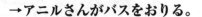

→アニルさんが部屋を出る。
Anil-san leaves the room.

→アニルさんがバスをおりる。
Anil-san gets off/leaves the bus.
* 〈place〉 includes vehicles.

Instead of を, から can also be used in the above sentences; whereas を focuses on the movement, から focuses on the idea of *out of*.

The reverse direction (the destination or goal of a movement) is indicated with に, for the verbs 入る *to go/come in, enter* and 乗る *to get/on, embark* (⇨L6GNⅥ):

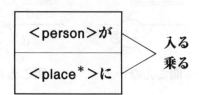

→アニルさんが部屋に入る。　*Anil-san enters the room.*

→アニルさんがバスに乗る。　*Anil-san gets on the bus.*
* 〈place〉 includes vehicles.

Ⅶ. 見える and 聞こえる: する verbs and なる verbs 〈4〉

見える and 聞こえる are なる verbs in that they focus on the result of an action or development. ⇨L9GNⅤ, L11GNⅢ

GN

Imagine that you are climbing a mountain with a friend; when you reach the top from where you command a view of the city below and the sea in the distance, you might comment to your friend:

「海が見える。」or
「海が見えます。」

I can see the sea.
(lit. The sea is visible).

In the silence of the mountains the song of the birds is very noticeable, prompting your comment:

「鳥の声が聞こえる。」or
「鳥の声が聞こえます。」

I can hear the song of the birds.
(lit. The song of the birds is audible).

This situation illustrates a change from 'not being visible/heard' to 'being visible/audible'.

見えない　　　　見える　　　　聞こえない　　　　聞こえる

The **する** verbs corresponding to **見える** and **聞こえる** are **見る** and **聞く**; **見える** and **聞こえる** are 《ーを verbs》 taking the following structure:

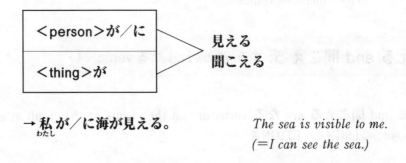

→ 私が／に海が見える。

The sea is visible to me.
(＝I can see the sea.)

98

→私が／に鳥の声が聞こえる。　　*The song of the birds is audible to me.*
　　　　　　　　　　　　　　　　　(＝I can hear the song of the birds.)

Note that ＜person＞が／に, and its topicalized forms ＜person＞は／には are often omitted.

Ⅷ. ところ＜1＞: *place, at/by (place)*

GN

ところ *place* is used in a variety of meanings: ⇨L23GNⅣ

1. **ここにおところとお名前を書いてください。**
   Please write your address and name here.

2. **静かなところで話しましょう。**
   Let's talk somewhere quiet.

3. **いろいろなところを見たいと思っています。**
   I'd like to see a lot of different places.

4. **わからないところがあったら、聞いてください。**
   Please ask if there's anything you don't understand.

＜place/person＞のところ indicates the place that something/someone is at or near.

5. **まどのところに田中さんがいます。**
   There is Tanaka-san at the window.

6. **歩道橋のところからかんばんが見えます。**
   A signboard can be seen from the footbridge.

7. **あとで私のところに来てください。**
   Please come to (see) me (at my office/place) later.

Make sure you don't omit 〜のところ in examples like 5. and 7. above:

！　× **まどに田中さんがいます。**
　　× **あとで私に来てください。**

The following illustrations show the difference that can obtain between an expression with and without 〜のところ:

まどに田中さんがいます。　　　まどのところに田中さんがいます。
　　た なか

In conversational language, ところ is sometimes shortened to とこ.

IX. 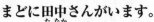 〈quantity/duration〉＋は: *at least*

Suppose 木村先生 and 山田先生 told you, respectively:
　　　き むらせんせい　　　やま だ せんせい

木村先生：毎日２時間勉強してください。
　　　　　まいにち　　じ かんべんきょう

山田先生：毎日２時間は勉強してください。

Which of the two teachers is stricter? The answer is 山田先生 because the discourse particle は when added to an expression of quantity or duration means *at least*. Therefore 木村先生 told you to study 2 hours a day, but 山田先生 told to study AT LEAST 2 hours a day!

1. A：駅からどのぐらいかかりますか。
　　　えき
   How long does it take from the station?

   B：２０分はかかると思います。
   　　にじゅっぷん　　　　　おも
   I think it takes a good 20 minutes.

2. １週間に１度は家族に手紙を書きます。
   　いっしゅうかん　　ど　　かぞく　てがみ　か
   I write a letter to my family at least once a week.

X. ～め: making ordinal numbers

Number ＋～め indicates the position within a series. ～め is often written using Kanji:「～目」

ひとり	one person	→	ひとりめ	the first (one/person)
2人 ふたり	two persons	→	2人め	the second (one/person)
ひとつ	one (thing)	→	ひとつめ	the first (one)
ふたつ	two (things)	→	ふたつめ	the second (one)
2か月 げつ	two months	→	2か月目 め	the second month
1年 ねん	one year	→	1年目 め	the first year

ひとつめのかど　　　　　　　　　　the first corner
みっつめの駅
えき　　　　　　　　　　the third stop/station

1番目のかど*
ばん　　　　　　　　　　the first corner
2番目の人
ひと　　　　　　　　　　the second person
　　* 1番：No.1

1. 左から3番目（3人目）の人が田中さんです。
ひだり　　　　にん　　　　たなか
The third person from the left is Tanaka-san.

2. ふたつめ（2番目）のかどを右に曲がってください。
みぎ　ま
Turn right at the second corner.

3. 日本に来て、まだ1週間目です。
にほん　き　　　いっしゅうかん め
This is still the first week since I came to Japan.

GN

Conversation Notes

<General Information>

1. Location and Landmarks

a. Location

In Lesson 4, we saw some basic expressions of location; here are some more:

手前	てまえ	*before*
先	さき	*beyond*
むかい		*across the street from*

交差点の手前
こうさてん

交差点の先

郵便局のむかい
ゆうびんきょく

① **銀行は、あの交差点の手前にあります。**
ぎんこう
The bank is before (you get to) that intersection.

② **銀行は、あの交差点の先です。**
The bank is beyond that intersection.

③ **銀行は、郵便局のむかいです。**
The bank is across the street from the post office.

b. Landmarks

Landmarks can be very useful for directions. Public buildings (schools, hospitals, post offices, police stations) or certain conspicuous buildings (very tall, black etc.) can be seen from almost anywhere and hence make useful landmarks.

A：まっすぐ行くと、けいさつがありますから、

Go straight, and you will find a police station.

B：けいさつって、police station ですね。

Keesatsu is a police station, isn't it?

A：ええ。銀行は、そのむかいですよ。

Yes. The bank is across the street from it.

To check if there are any landmarks, ask:

その近くに何か目印になるものがありますか。

Is there a landmark nearby?

[Typical landmarks]

警察	けいさつ	*police station*
交番	こうばん	*police box*
消防署	しょうぼうしょ	*fire station*
郵便局	ゆうびんきょく	*post office*
市役所	しやくしょ	*municipal office*
お寺	おてら	*temple*
神社	じんじゃ	*shrine*

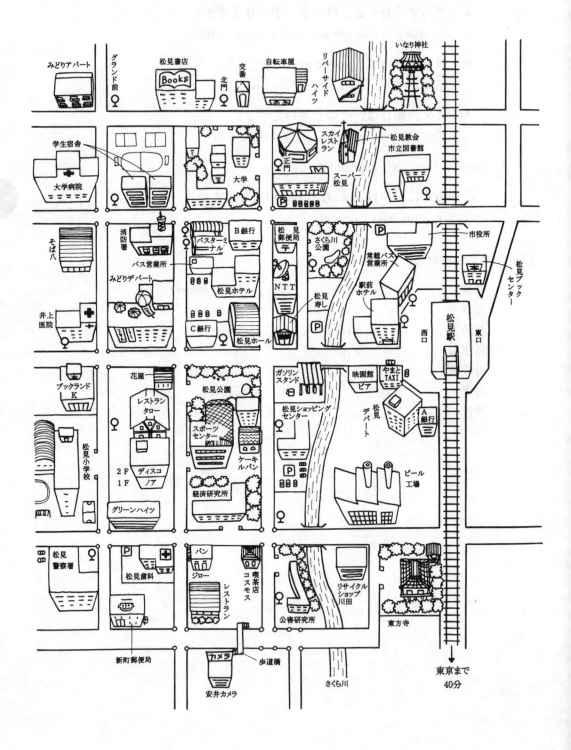

<Strategies>

S-1. How to ask for directions

You can ask for directions using the following expressions:

すみません。＜destination＞へ行きたいんですけど／が。↘
Excuse me. How do I get to ＜destination＞?

あのう、すみません。＜destination＞（は）┃どこですか。
Excuse me. Where is ＜destination＞?　　　　　　┃どこでしょうか。

① すみません。安井カメラへ行きたいんですけど……
　　やすい
Excuse me. How do I get to Yasui Camera?

② あのう、すみません。NTT はどこですか。
Excuse me. Where's NTT?

S-2. How to give directions

The following expressions can be used to give someone else directions for getting to a place:

a. [V-te] ください。

 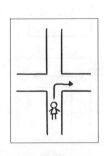 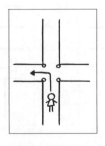 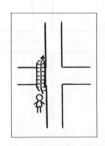

まっすぐ　　　　右に曲がって　　信号を左に　　　歩道橋を渡って
　　　　　　　　みぎ　ま　　　　しんごう　ひだり　　ほどうきょう　わた
行ってください。くださ。　　　　曲がってください。ください。

b. ＜action＞て、＜position＞ $\begin{vmatrix} 。 \\ です。 \end{vmatrix}$

① **右に曲がって、左。**
みぎ ま ひだり
Turn right, (and you will find it) on the left.

② **まっすぐ行って、左です。**
い
Go straight, (and you'll see it) on the left.

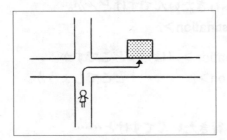 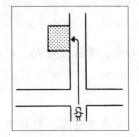

c. ＜action 1＞て、＜action 2＞てください。

① **まっすぐ行って、交差点を右に曲がってください。**
こうさてん
Go straight, then turn right at the intersection.

② **歩道橋を渡って、まっすぐ行ってください。**
ほどうきょう わた
Cross the footbridge, then go straight on.

③ **その交差点を右に曲がって、50m ぐらいまっすぐ行ってください。**
Turn right at that intersection, then go straight for about 50 m.

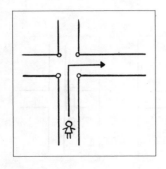 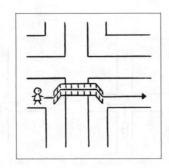 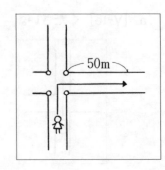

d. ＜landmark＞を＜action＞と、│＜position＞にあります。
　　　　　　　　　　　　　　　│＜target building＞が見えます。

① 交差点を左に曲がると、右側にあります。
If you turn left at the intersection, you'll see it on the right.

② その信号を右に行くと、20m ぐらい先に銀行があります。
If you turn right at the traffic light, you will see the bank some 20m from there.

③ その角を右に曲がると、NTT が見えますよ。
If you turn right at the corner, you'll see NTT.

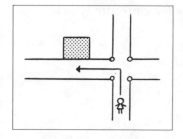
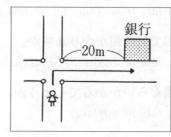
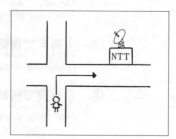

e. To give a position relative to a landmark, proceed as follows:

　　＜landmark＞（は）、わかりますか。
　　＜destination＞は、＜landmark＞の＜position＞です。

　　A：銀行はどこでしょうか。　　　　　*Where is the bank?*

　　B：ええと、NTT は、わかりますか。　*Well, do you know where NTT is?*

　　A：はい。　　　　　　　　　　　　　*Yes.*

　　B：銀行はそのとなりです。　　　　　*The bank is next to it.*

S-3. How to go by public transport

a. Asking how long it takes to get to a place.

<starting point>から

<target>まで + どのくらいかかるでしょうか。
どのくらいかかります。↗
何時間かかるでしょうか。
何時間かかりますか。

<transport means>で

① 天王台の駅から大学までバスでどのくらいかかりますか。
How long does it take from Tennodai station to the university by bus?

② 大阪まで新幹線で何時間かかりますか。
How long does it take to Osaka by Shinkansen?

③ 飛行機で何時間ぐらいかかるでしょうか。
How long does it take by airplane?

④ 歩いて、どのくらいかかるでしょうか。
How long does it take on foot?

b. Asking how to get there.

<target> に／まで行きたいんですが 、どう行ったらいいでしょうか。
まで

(I'd) like to go to ⟨target⟩, how do I get there?

① 秋葉原まで行きたいんですが、どう行ったらいいでしょうか。
I'd like to go Akihabara, how do I get there?

② 横浜大学まで、どう行ったらいいでしょうか。
How do I get to Yokohama University?

c. Telling others how to get there.

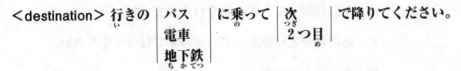

＜destination＞で、｜電車／バス｜を降ります。

① 天王台で、電車を降ります。
You get off the train at Tennodai ⟨station⟩.

② 大手町で、バスを降ります。
You get off the bus at Otemachi.

CN

＜destination＞行きの｜バス／電車／地下鉄｜に乗って｜次／2つ目｜で降りてください。

天王台行きのバスに乗って、3つ目で降りてください。
Take the bus to Tennodai and get off at the 3rd stop.

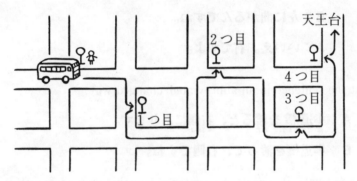

＜station＞で～線に乗り換えてください。

大手町で、千代田線に乗り換えてください。
Change to the Chiyoda-Line at Otemachi ⟨station⟩.

S-4. How to confirm information —2.

a. Repeat a sentence or key word and add **んですね** ↗ .

① A：右に曲がると、歩道橋があります。
みぎ　ま　　　　　　ほどうきょう

B：右に曲がるんですね。↗

② A：あの角を左に曲がって、まっすぐ行ってください。
かど　ひだり　　　　　　　　い

B：左に曲がって、まっすぐ行くんですね。↗

③ A：あの角を左に曲がって、まっすぐ行ってください。

B：まっすぐですね。↗

④ A：右に曲がると、歩道橋があります。

B：左に曲がるんですね。↗

A：いいえ。右ですよ。

b. Repeat the sentence in an abbreviated/changed way:

A：歩道橋を渡ると、右側にあります。
ほどうきょう　わた　　　みぎがわ

B：歩道橋を渡って、右側ですね。↗

In this example, B repeats A's sentence from his own perspective.

A：右に曲がると、銀行がありますから、その前です。
　　ま　　　　　ぎんこう　　　　　　　まえ

〇 B：右に曲がって、銀行の前ですね。

✕ B：右に曲がって、銀行の前にあるんですね。

110

まとめ 3

A. GRAMMAR

Ⅰ. Units of time

Ⅱ. Summary of **-te** forms

Ⅲ. Summary of particles

Ⅳ. The verb する

Ⅴ. が and は: が used to select a subject

B. CONVERSATION

Ⅰ. Summary of Conversational Strategies

Ⅱ. Additional Information
 1. Use of けっこうです
 2. *Aizuchi*
 3. Use of そう

A. Grammar

The following is a list of units of time; note how they combine with numbers and question words:

	秒（びょう）second	分（ふん）minute	時間（じかん）hour
1	1秒（いちびょう）	1分（いっぷん）	1時間（いちじかん）
2	2秒（にびょう）	2分（にふん）	2時間（にじかん）
3	3秒（さんびょう）	3分（さんぷん）	3時間（さんじかん）
4	4秒（よんびょう）	4分（よんぷん）	4時間（よじかん）
5	5秒（ごびょう）	5分（ごふん）	5時間（ごじかん）
6	6秒（ろくびょう）	6分（ろっぷん）	6時間（ろくじかん）
7	7秒（ななびょう）（しちびょう）	7分（ななふん）（しちふん）	7時間（ななじかん）（しちじかん）
8	8秒（はちびょう）	8分（はっぷん）（はちふん）	8時間（はちじかん）
9	9秒（きゅうびょう）	9分（きゅうふん）	9時間（くじかん）
10	10秒（じゅうびょう）	10分（じっぷん）（じゅっぷん）	10時間（じゅうじかん）
?	何秒（なんびょう）	何分（なんぷん）	何時間（なんじかん）

	日（ひ）day	週（しゅう）week
1	1日（いちにち）	1週間（いっしゅうかん）
2	2日（ふつか）	2週間（にしゅうかん）
3	3日（みっか）	3週間（さんしゅうかん）
4	4日（よっか）	4週間（よんしゅうかん）
5	5日（いつか）	5週間（ごしゅうかん）
6	6日（むいか）	6週間（ろくしゅうかん）
7	7日（なのか）	7週間（ななしゅうかん）
8	8日（ようか）	8週間（はっしゅうかん）
9	9日（ここのか）	9週間（きゅうしゅうかん）
10	10日（とおか）	10週間（じっしゅうかん）（じゅっしゅうかん）
11	11日（じゅういちにち）	
14	14日（じゅうよっか）	
20	20日（はつか）	
24	24日（にじゅうよっか）	
?	何日（なんにち）	何週間（なんしゅうかん）

112

	月（つき） month		年（ねん／とし） year
1	1か月（いっかげつ）	1月（ひとつき）	1年（いちねん）
2	2か月（にかげつ）	2月（ふたつき）	2年（にねん）
3	3か月（さんかげつ）	3月（みつき）	3年（さんねん）
4	4か月（よんかげつ）		4年（よねん）
5	5か月（ごかげつ）		5年（ごねん）
6	6か月（ろっかげつ）	半年（はんとし）	6年（ろくねん）
7	7か月（ななかげつ） （しちかげつ）		7年（ななねん） （しちねん）
8	8か月（はちかげつ） （はっかげつ）		8年（はちねん）
9	9か月（きゅうかげつ）		9年（きゅうねん）
10	10か月（じっかげつ） （じゅっかげつ）		10年（じゅうねん）
?	何か月（なんかげつ）		何年（なんねん）

半時間（はんじかん）（＝30分）	half an hour
半日（はんにち）	half a day
半月（はんつき）	half a month
半年（はんとし）	six months, half a year
1時間半（いちじかんはん）	one and a half hours
1か月半（いっかげつはん）	one and a half months
2年半（にねんはん）	two and a half years

まとめ

Ⅱ. Summary of -te forms

		Plain non-past	-te form	Negative -te form	
N o u n	[N]	学生だ がくせい かばんだ	学生で かばんで	学生じゃなくて かばんじゃなくて	
A d j e c t i v e	[NA]	便利だ べんり 静かだ しず	便利で 静かで	便利じゃなくて 静かじゃなくて	
	[A]	高い たか 大きい おお 寒い さむ 痛い いた	高くて 大きくて 寒くて 痛くて	高くなくて 大きくなくて 寒くなくて 痛くなくて	
V e r b	[V] Ⅰ	聞く き 急ぐ いそ 飲む の 呼ぶ よ 死ぬ し 話す はな 買う か 帰る かえ 待つ ま 行く い	聞いて 急いで 飲んで 呼んで 死んで 話して 買って 帰って 待って 行って	聞かなくて 急がなくて 飲まなくて 呼ばなくて 死ななくて 話さなくて 買わなくて 帰らなくて 待たなくて 行かなくて	聞かないで 急がないで 飲まないで 呼ばないで 死なないで 話さないで 買わないで 帰らないで 待たないで 行かないで
	Ⅱ	食べる た 見る み	食べて 見て	食べなくて 見なくて	食べないで 見ないで
	Ⅲ	来る く する	来て き して	来なくて こ しなくて	来ないで こ しないで

Uses:

1) [V-te] ください。

    1. ちょっと待ってください。   *Wait a moment, please.*

    2. あした来てください。   *Please come tomorrow.*

2) [V-te]、～

    1. 食堂に行って、昼ごはんを食べ   *(I)'ll go to a cafeteria and (then) eat lunch.*
      ます。

    2. 名前を書いて、はんこを押してく   *Please write your name and put your seal*
      ださい。   *here.*

3) [V-te] います。

    1. お金が落ちています。   *There's some money (that has been dropped).*

    2. ドアが開いています。   *The door's open.*

4) [V-te] いません。

    1. まだ新聞を読んでいません。   *(I) haven't read the newspaper.*

    2. まだごはんを食べていません。   *(I) haven't eaten yet.*

5) [V-te] から、～

    1. 授業が終わってから、本屋に行   *(I)'ll go to the bookshop after class is over.*
      きます。

    2. 家へ帰ってから、何をしますか。   *What will you do after returning home?*

6) [V-te] もいいです。

    1. ここでたばこをすってもいいです   *May I smoke here?*
      か。

    2. 英語で書いてもいいです。   *You may write in English.*

7) [A-kute] / [NA] で、～
   [A-nakute] / [NA] じゃなくて、～

    1. この辞書は古くて、小さいです。   *This dictionary is old and small.*

    2. 地下鉄は便利で、安くて、はやい   *The subway is convenient, cheap and fast.*
      です。

3. このレストランはあまり高くなくて、おいしいです。

This restaurant isn't very expensive and the food is good.

8) [N]で、〜

1. 木村先生はこの大学の先生で、私の指導教官です。

Kimura-sensee is a teacher of this university and my academic adviser.

2. 鈴木さんは学生で、独身です。

Suzuki-san is a student and single.

Ⅲ. Summary of particles

1. が

1) (◁|||||◁ subject particle)

1. だれが行きますか。 *Who will go?*

2. (あそこに)田中さんがいます。 *There's Tanaka-san (over there).*

3. 私の国のほうが大きいです。 *My country is bigger.*

4. 鳥の声が聞こえます。 *The song of birds can be heard.*

5. ビールが飲みたいです。 *I want to drink beer.*

2) (⊂⊃ 〜, but 〜)

日本語はむずかしいですが、おもしろいです。
Japanese is difficult but interesting.

2. を

1) (◁|||||◁ object particle)

切手を買います。 *I buy stamps.*

2) (◁|||||◁ particle indicating the route)

バスは大学の前を通ります。 *The bus passes in front of the university.*

3) (◁|||||◁ particle indicating the place from which one leaves)

1. バスを降ります。 *I get off the bus.*

2. 部屋を出ます。 *I go out of the room.*

3. に

1) (🐟 particle of goal)

1. あした東京に行きます。   *I'll go to Tokyo tomorrow.*

2. 友だちに手紙を出します。   *I'll mail a letter to my friend.*

3. 友だちにプレゼントをあげます。   *I'll give a present to my friend.*

4. バスに乗ります。   *I'll get on the bus.*

5. 部屋に入ります。   *I'll enter the room.*

6. ここに名前を書いてください。   *Please write your name here.*

7. きのう駅で友だちに会いました。*I met my friend at the station yesterday.*

2) (🐟 particle of source)

友だちにプレゼントをもらいました。   *I received a present from my friend.*

3) (🐟 particle of location)

教室に電話があります。   *There's a telephone in the classroom.*

4) (🐟 time particle)

毎晩11時に寝ます。   *I go to bed at 11 o'clock every night.*

5) (🐟 with 見える／聞こえる)

A：海が見えますか。   *Can you see the sea?*

B：私には見えませんが。   *No, I can't see it.*

6) (🐟 particle indicating frequency per unit)

週に1回部屋をそうじします。 *I clean the room once a week.*

4. で

1) (🐟 particle of place of action)

1. 図書館で本を読みます。   *I read books in the library.*

2. 大学の前で会いましょう。   *Let's meet in front of the university.*

3. 新宿で地下鉄に乗ってください。 *Take the subway at Shinjuku.*

2 ）（ 🐟 particle of means）

1. はしで食べます。　　　　　　　*I eat with chopsticks.*

2. 車で帰りましょう。　　　　　　*Let's return by car.*

3. 航空便でいくらですか。　　　　*How much is it by airmail?*

4. 日本語で話してください。　　　*Please speak in Japanese.*

3 ）（ 🐟 particle of extent）

1. これは全部でいくらですか。　　*How much are these in all?*

2. A：だれと行きますか。　　　　*With whom will you go?*

   B：一人で行きます。　　　　　*I'll go alone.*

3. 3日でレポートを書きました。　*I wrote a report in three days.*

4. ロペスさんはクラスで一番せが高いです。

   Lopez-san is the tallest in the class.

5. へ　（ 🐟 direction particle）

先月日本へ来ました。　　　　　　*I came to Japan last month.*

6. と

1 ）（ ⚭ noun *and* noun）

田中さんと山下さんは友だちです。
Tanaka-san and Yamashita-san are friends.

2 ）（ 🐟 companion particle）

田中さんは山下さんと（いっしょに）映画を見ました。
Tanaka-san saw a movie (together) with Yamashita-san.

3 ）（ 🐟 particle of quotation）

1. 田中さんはあした東京に行くと言っています。
Tanaka-san says she will go to Tokyo tomorrow.

2. 漢字はおもしろいと思います。
I think Kanji are interesting.

4 ）（ ⊗⊗　 *if/when/whenever ~* ）

もう少し行くと、本屋があります。
If you go a little further, you will find a bookshop.

7. から

1 ）（ ⊲⊞⊞⊞⊂　 particle indicating the source）

友だちからプレゼントをもらいました。
I received a present from my friend.

2 ）（ ⊲⊞⊞⊞⊂　 particle indicating the starting time and point）

1. 私はインドから来ました。
I have come from India.

2. 9時から始めましょう。
Let's begin at (from) 9 o'clock.

3. 広島から東京まで何時間かかりますか。
How many hours does it take from Hiroshima to Tokyo?

3 ）（ ⊗⊗　 *because ~* ）

暗くなりましたから、帰りましょう。
It's become dark, so let's go home.

4 ）（ ⊗⊗　 *after ~* ）

授業が終わってから、本屋に行きます。
I'll go to the bookshop after class is over.

8. まで

1 ）（ ⊲⊞⊞⊞⊂　 particle indicating end-time/point）

1. 大阪まで車で行きました。
I went to Osaka by car.

2. きのうの晩は12時まで勉強しました。
I studied till 12 o'clock last night.

119

Ⅳ. The verb する

We saw that する means *to do, to make*; depending on its meaning, する takes a different structure:

1. する meaning *to make*

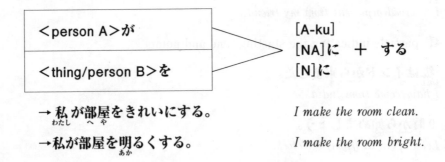

→ 私が部屋をきれいにする。　　　　*I make the room clean.*

→ 私が部屋を明るくする。　　　　　*I make the room bright.*

2. する meaning *to do*

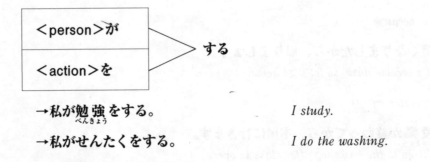

→ 私が勉強をする。　　　　　　　*I study.*

→ 私がせんたくをする。　　　　　*I do the washing.*

3. Verbal noun ＋する meaning *to do VN*

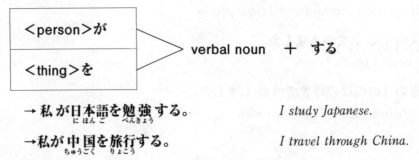

→ 私が日本語を勉強する。　　　　*I study Japanese.*

→ 私が中国を旅行する。　　　　　*I travel through China.*

The following are some of the **verbal noun ＋する** verbs we have learnt in Lessons 1 to 12.

勉強する	to study	注文する	to order (food, etc.)
洗濯する	to do the washing	質問する	to ask questions
旅行する	to travel, make a trip	食事する	to eat a meal
予約する	to reserve	掃除する	to clean, to hoover
相談する	to consult	結婚する	to get married
出席する	to attend	欠席する	to be absent
入院する	to be hospitalized	診察する	to examine a patient
心配する	to worry	買物する	to shop
連絡する	to contact	運転する	to drive
散歩する	to take a walk	説明する	to explain
約束する	to promise	予習する	to prepare (a lesson)
注意する	to be careful	準備する	to prepare
電話する	to telephone	テニスする	to play tennis

まとめ

You can use the structure particle **を** as an object particle after a verbal noun: **勉強をする**, **買物をする**, etc.

There is no difference in meaning with or without **を**; note, however, that **を** is not used twice in the same sentence.

1. 毎日勉強<u>を</u>します。＝毎日勉強します。 *I study everyday.*

2. 日本語の勉強<u>を</u>します。＝日本語<u>を</u>勉強します。 *I study Japanese.*

⚠ ✕ 日本語<u>を</u>勉強<u>を</u>します。

3. 大学ではどんな勉強<u>を</u>していますか。
What are you studying at university?

4. する meaning *to decide, to choose*

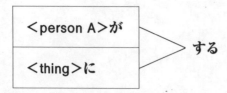

121

→ 私 がコーヒーにする。   *I'll have coffee.*

→ 私がこのカメラにする。   *I'll take this camera.*

A：何にしますか。   *What will you have?*

B：コーヒーにします。   *I'll have coffee.*

V. が and は: が used to select a subject

We saw that は indicates something with which speaker and listener are familiar, whereas が is used to inform the listener of something new. ⇨ まとめ1AV, 2AⅧ

Look at the cartoons (A) and (B).

(A) Anil-san is looking for Ogawa-san. He asks one person whether he is Ogawa-san, but that person answers that his name is Yamada. Yamada-san then informs Anil-san that the person telephoning is Ogawa-san.

Yamada-san uses は in his answer 「私は山田です。」, whereas he uses が to inform Anil-san about the identity of Ogawa-san: 「あの人が小川さんですよ。」

(B) Anil-san is trying to find Kyoto on the map. He asks Tanaka-san whether the place he is pointing at is Kyoto, saying 「ここは京都ですか。」. Tanaka-san tells him that isn't Kyoto but Tokyo, and goes on, point out Kyoto with the words 「ここが京都ですよ。」

ここが, therefore, functions as a subject that is new to the listener. Yamada-san in cartoon (A) picks one person in the crowd and says that the person over there (as distinct from other persons) is Ogawa-san.

この人
その人 ｝ が　小川さんです。
あの人

Likewise, Tanaka-san in cartoon (B) picks one place out of many others and says that this place (not any other place) is Kyoto.

ここ
そこ ｝ が　京都です。
あそこ

（A）

（B）

B. Conversation

I. *Summary of Conversational Strategies*

1. Factual information

☐ ☐ How to explain your symptoms　　　：頭が痛いんです。
　　　　　　　　⇨L9 S-1　　　　　　　あたま　いた

☐ ☐ How to ask for instructions on　　　：これは何の薬ですか。
taking a medicine　　⇨L9 S-3　　　　　　なん　くすり

☐ ☐ How to find what you want　　　　：＜colour/size, etc.＞の[N]ありますか。
　　　　　　　　⇨L10 S-1

☐ ☐ How to ask for something to be　　：〜っていう[N]が見つからないんです
done for you　　　⇨L11 S-1　　　けど。　　　　　み

☐ ☐ How to ask for directions　　　　：〜はどこでしょうか。
　　　　　　　　⇨L12 S-1　　　　〜へ行きたいんですけど。

☐ ☐ How to give directions　　　　　：まっすぐ行ってください。
　　　　　　　　　　　　　　　　　　い
　　　　　　　　⇨L12 S-2　　　　まっすぐ行って、右に曲がってください。
　　　　　　　　　　　　　　　　　　　　みぎ　まが
　　　　　　　　　　　　　　　　〜て、＜location＞です。
　　　　　　　　　　　　　　　　〜と、＜location＞にあります。

☐ ☐ How to go by public transport
　　　　　　　　⇨L12 S-3

(a) Asking how long it takes to　　：〜から〜までどのくらいかかるでしょう
get there　　　　　　　　　　か。／何時間かかりますか。
　　　　　　　　　　　　　　　　　　　　　　なんじかん
(b) Asking how to get there　　　：＜target＞に／まで行きたいんですが,
　　　　　　　　　　　　　　　　どう行ったらいいでしょうか。

☐ ☐ How to confirm information ─2.　：右に曲がると、歩道橋があります。
　　　　　　　　　　　　　　　　　　　　　　　ほどうきょう
　　　　　　　　⇨L12 S-4　　　　─右に曲がるんですね↗

2. Judgement

☐ ☐ How to consult a doctor ⇨L9 S-2　：〜ても　　　｜いいでしょうか。
　　　　　　　　　　　　　　　　〜なくても　｜

☐ ☐ How to ask for advice　　　　　：[N]は私には、[A/NA]でしょうか。
　　　　　　　　　　　　　　　　　　わたし
　　　　　　　　⇨L10 S-2　　　　[N1]と[N2]とどちらがいいかしら。
　　　　　　　　　　　　　　　　＜group＞の中でどれが一番いいかな。
　　　　　　　　　　　　　　　　　　　なか　　　　いちばん

3. Emotions

4. Actions

☐ ☐ How to find what you want   ：＜colour/size/design＞の[N]
             ⇨L10 S-1   （を）見せてください。

☐ ☐ How to order a book   ⇨L11 S-2 ：注文、お願いします。

☐ ☐ How to cancel your order   ：悪いんですけど、注文取り消したいん
             ⇨L11 S-3   ですが。

5. Social formulas

☐ ☐ How to decline politely⇨L10 S-3 ：ううん……。↘

                     そうですね。でも。↘

                     ちょっと。～ほうがいいんですけど。

                     またにします。

6. Communication strategies

☐ ☐ How to confirm information —2.   ：～んですね。
             ⇨L12 S-4

    (a) Repeating a key word

☐ ☐ Aizuchi   ⇨まとめ3BⅡ2：はい／ええ／そうですね。

まとめ

II. *Additional Information*

1. Uses of けっこうです

You have already come across several uses of **けっこうです**; here is a review:

① シャルマ：これでいいですか。 *Is this all right?*

　　事務員：はい、けっこうです。 *Yes, that's all right.* 〈L6〉

② シャルマ：ええと、はんこは持ってないんですけど。
　　　　　　　Well, I don't have a seal.

　　事務員：じゃ、サインでけっこうです。 ⇨L6CN S-5
　　　　　　You can sign instead, then.

③ 田　中：出版社がわからないんですけど。 〈L11〉
　　　　　　I don't know the publisher's name.

　　店　員：あ、けっこうですよ。
　　　　　　Oh, that's all right./It doesn't matter.

Now look at the following:

④ 田　中：どのくらいかかりますか。
　　　　　　How long will it take?

　　店　員：2週間で入ると思いますけど。
　　　　　　I think it'll come in two weeks.

　　田　中：2週間ですか。じゃ、けっこうです。
　　　　　　Two weeks! It's all right, then.

⑤ ウェートレス：お飲み物はいかがですか。
　　　　　　　　Would you like something to drink?

　　客：いえ、けっこうです。
　　　　No, I'm O.K./No, thanks.

Like English *all right*, **けっこうです** can mean *(Yes) that's fine, that's all right* (examples ①～③), but can also be used for refusal *(No) it's all right, (No) thank you* (examples ④ and ⑤). It is normally clear from the situation (and preceding words like **はい、いいえ、じゃ**, etc.) which meaning is intended.

2. *Aizuchi*

Successful communication depends on cooperation between listener and speaker, to help along the conversation and avoid periods of silence. As a listener, it is important that you indicate your interest in what's being said; in Japanese, **あいづち** *(Aizuchi)* is an important device for doing just that.

あいづち signals that the listener is paying attention and wishes the conversation to continue. The most common *Aizuchi* are **はい** (↘) or **ええ** (↘) and **うん** (↘).
⇨L1CN4

Unlike in English, where the speaker will get irritated if too many *yeahs* and *hmms* are thrown in, **あいづち** in Japanese are extremely frequent, occurring after almost each phrase or sentence said by the speaker. The speaker will often even encourage the listener to give **あいづち** by slowing down the last part of a phrase and giving it a dangling intonation.

① A：右に曲がると、駅がありますから ↘ 銀行は駅の前ですよ。↘

B：　　　　　　　　　　　　　　　　はい。　　　　　　そうですか。

② A：橋を渡って、左に行くと ↘ 白い建物が見えますから ↘ すぐわかります。

B：　　　　　　　　　　はい。　　　　　　　　　　はい。

3. Uses of そう

You have already come across several uses of **そう**: here is a review (in the examples below, **そう** refers to the underlined parts):

1. Refers to something that has been mentioned and is understood by the listener:

① A：事務室って、センターの事務室ですか。

B：ええ、そうです。

② A：きょうは、寒いですね。

B：そうですね。

2. Used to confirm the actions of the listener:

① A：私が、電話しましょうか。

B：すみません。そうしてください。

② A：その角を右に曲がってください。

B：右ですね。

A：ええ、そうすると、右側にありますよ。

喫茶店で
きっさてん
At a coffee shop

OBJECTIVES:

GRAMMAR

Ⅰ. 好きだ／きらいだ／上手だ／下手だ
　　　　　　　　じょうず　　へた
Ⅱ. あげる／さしあげる
　　もらう／いただく ⎫
　　　　　　　　　　　⎬ : giving and receiving〈1〉
　　くれる／くださる ⎭
Ⅲ. Noun modification〈2〉
Ⅳ. 〜ている〈2〉 *be V-ing*: progressive action
Ⅴ. 〜ばかりだ: *(only) just* 〜
Ⅵ. ＜quantity/duration＞＋も: *as many/long as*

CONVERSATION

＜General Information＞
1. Introductions —3.
2. Building a relationship in a conversation

＜Strategies＞
S-1. How to apologize and give an excuse
S-2. How to confirm what you heard from someone
S-3. How to bring up the main topic
S-4. How to make and accept an offer
S-5. How to express modesty

Model Conversation

Characters ：Lisa Brown, Tanaka(田中), Suzuki(鈴木)

Situation ：Tanaka-san and Lisa-san are waiting in a coffee shop for Suzuki-san, who is an assistant in the computer science department. Suzuki-san arrives late and Tanaka-san introduces Lisa-san to him. When Tanaka-san reminds Suzuki-san to give her information about a second-hand shop where Lisa-san can buy a cheap T.V., Suzuki-san offers his own old set to Lisa-san.

Flow-chart ：

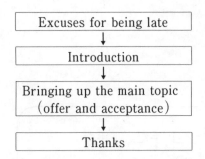

```
┌─────────────────────────────┐
│   Excuses for being late     │
└─────────────────────────────┘
              ↓
┌─────────────────────────────┐
│       Introduction           │
└─────────────────────────────┘
              ↓
┌─────────────────────────────┐
│ Bringing up the main topic   │
│  (offer and acceptance)      │
└─────────────────────────────┘
              ↓
┌─────────────────────────────┐
│         Thanks               │
└─────────────────────────────┘
```

―喫茶店で―

鈴　木：やあ。ごめん、ごめん。遅くなっちゃって。

田　中：あ、こんにちは。

鈴　木：先生たちと昼飯くってたもんだから。

田　中：すみません、お忙しいのに。

鈴　木：いえ、いえ。かまわないんですよ。

田　中：あの、鈴木さん。こちら、この間お話ししたリサ・ブラウンさん。

ブラウン：リサ・ブラウンです。よろしくお願いします。

鈴　木：こちらこそ。鈴木です。
　　　　おうわさは山下くんからいつも聞いています。

ブラウン：えっ、どんなことかしら。

鈴　木：いや。まあ、日本語が上手だとか、いろいろなことですけど。

ブラウン：えっ、そんなこと。

　　　　　　＊　　　　　＊　　　　　＊

田　中：あのう、ところで、テレビのことなんですが。

鈴　木：ああ、そうそう。
　　　　ブラウンさん、リサイクルの安い店、さがしているんですって。

130

ブラウン：ええ。
鈴　木：それなら、ぼくのをあげてもいいですよ。
ブラウン：えっ、そんな。
鈴　木：ぼくは、この間、新しいの買ったばかりだから。
ブラウン：でも、よろしいんですか。
鈴　木：どうぞ使ってください。
ブラウン：(To Tanaka-san) いいのかしら、いただいても。
田　中：うん。いただいたら。
鈴　木：実は、2台もあって、困ってたんですよ。
ブラウン：そうですか。それじゃ、えんりょなくいただきます。
鈴　木：よかった、お役に立てて。
ブラウン：ありがとうございます。
田　中：よかったわね。

Report

<田中さんの日記>

　きょう、リサさんを鈴木さんに紹介した。鈴木さんは、先生と食事をしていて、20分も遅れてきた。いつも時間に遅れる人だ。リサさんが中古のテレビを買いたいと言ったので、鈴木さんに頼んだ。ところが、鈴木さんはテレビを2台持っているから、古いのをリサさんにあげると言った。鈴木さんはいつもお金がないと言っているのだが、リサさんには、とても親切だった。

New Words and Expressions

Words in the conversation

喫茶店	きっさてん	*coffee shop*
昼飯	ひるめし	*lunch* ＝昼ご飯
くう		*to eat* (male informal form)
忙しい	いそがしい	*busy*
この間	このあいだ	*the other day, few days ago*
うわさ		*rumour, hearsay*
上手 (な)	じょうず (な)	*good at, skilful*
リサイクルの店	リサイクルのみせ	*second-hand shop*
ところで		*by the way*
～台	～だい	*counter for machines, cars or TV sets*
いただく		*to get, to receive* (polite equivalent of もらう)
実は	じつは	*in fact*
えんりょ		*reserve, hesitation*

<Expressions in the conversation>

ごめん。 ＝ごめんなさい。　　　　　　　*I am sorry.*

遅くなっちゃって。　　　　　　　　　*I'm late.*

This phrase is a casual contraction of **遅くなってしまって** ⇨L22GN　**ごめん。遅くなっちゃって。** is an inversion of **遅くなっちゃって、ごめん。** *I'm sorry I'm late.*

昼飯くってたもんだから。　　　　　　*Because I was eating lunch.*

もんだから is casual for **ものですから**. **もの** *thing* is used in many ways; here it explains a reason or cause. ⇨CN

すみません、お忙しいのに。　　　　　*Excuse me for taking up your time.*

This is an inversion of **お忙しいのに、すみません。** **～のに** means *although, in spite of.*

かまわないんですよ。　　　　　　　　*It's all right, I don't mind.*

132

おうわさは山下くんからいつも聞いています。 — *I often hear about you from Yamashita.*

えっ、そんなこと。 — *Really? I don't deserve that...* ⇨S-2

ところで、テレビのことなんですけど。 — *By the way, about the TV.*
　　ところで indicates that you are coming to the point. ⇨S-3

ああ、そうそう。 — *Oh, right.*

そんな。↗ — *I can't accept that, that's too much.*

新しいの買ったばかりだから。 — *I've just bought a new one.*

でも、よろしいんですか。 — *Are you sure it's all right?*
　　よろしい is the polite for いい.

いただいたら。↗ — *Why don't you accept it?*
　　Short for いただいたら、どうですか or いただいたら、いいでしょう.

えんりょなくいただきます。 — *make so bold as to accept.*

よかった、お役に立てて。 — *Glad to be of help.*
　　Inversion of お役に立てて、よかった.
　　cf. お役に立てて、うれしいです。*I am happy to ～.*

よかったわね。 — *I'm glad for you/Congratulations!*
　　When hearing good news about someone, you can congratulate him/her with
　　「よかったね。／わね。」; for commiseration,「ざんねんだったね。／わね。
　　(What a pity)」or「たいへんだったね。／わね。*(You've had a hard time)*」
　　can be used.

Words in the report

紹介する	しょうかいする	to introduce
食事	しょくじ	meal
時間	じかん	time
遅れる	おくれる	to be late
中古	ちゅうこ	used
頼む	たのむ	to ask
親切（な）	しんせつ（な）	kind
ところが		however
いつも		always

Grammar Notes

I. 好きだ／きらいだ／上手だ／下手だ

Examples

①　私は音楽が好きです。
I like music.

②　田中さんはピアノが上手です。
Tanaka-san is good at playing the piano.

【*Explanation*】

好きだ and きらいだ are **na** adjectives meaning *to be fond of, to like* and *to dislike*. Things/persons one likes or dislikes are indicated by が. 上手だ *to be good at* and 下手だ *to be poor at* also take the same structure:

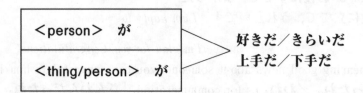

→私がやさいが好きだ。
I like vegetables.

→鈴木さんがテニスが上手だ。
Suzuki-san is good at tennis.

Ⅱ. あげる／さしあげる
もらう／いただく　: giving and receiving〈1〉
くれる／くださる

Examples

① 鈴木さんはリサさんにテレビをあげました。
Suzuki-san gave Lisa-san a TV.

② リサさんは鈴木さんにテレビをもらいました。
Lisa-san received a TV from Suzuki-san.

③ 鈴木さんは私にテレビをくれました。
Suzuki-san gave me a TV.

④ リサさんは先生に手紙をいただきました。
Lisa-san received a letter from her teacher.

【Explanation】   ⇨L3GN I

There are three types of verbs expressing the idea of giving & receiving in Japanese:

1. The **あげる** *(give outgroup)* type
2. The **もらう** *(receive)* type
3. The **くれる** *(give ingroup)* type

GN

1. The あげる *(give outgroup)* type

The structure of the **あげる** type is as follows:

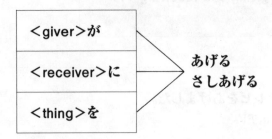

→鈴木さんがリサさんにテレビをあげる。
Suzuki-san gives Lisa-san a TV.

→私がアニルさんにテープをあげる。
I give Anil-san a tape.

When the receiver is of higher social status than the giver, **さしあげる** is used; when the receiver is of equal or lower social status than the giver, **あげる** is used:

あげる　（receiver is equal/inferior to giver）

私はリサさんに本をあげました。
I gave Lisa-san a book.

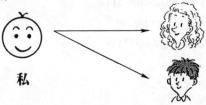

さしあげる　（receiver is superior to giver）

私は先生に本をさしあげました。
I gave my teacher a book.

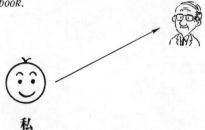

When giving food/drink to animals (or water to plants), and also when giving to one's younger brothers/sisters, **やる** is considered more appropriate than **あげる**, especially by older speakers.

さしあげる is never used when referring to family members; therefore only **あげる**（or **やる** for giving to junior members）can be used for giving to a family member:

　　○　私は父に時計をあげました。　　*I gave father a watch.*

　　×　私は父に時計をさしあげました。

2．The もらう *(receive)* type

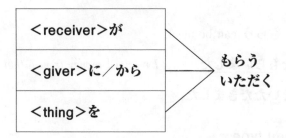

→リサさんが鈴木さんにテレビをもらう。
Lisa-san receives a TV from Suzuki-san.

→私がアニルさんから本をもらう。
I receive a book from Anil-san.

When the giver is superior to the receiver, **いただく** is used:

> **もらう**　（giver is equal/inferior to receiver）

私は田中さんに手紙をもらいました。
I received a letter from Tanaka-san.

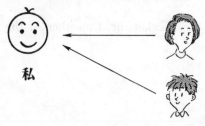

私

いただく （giver is superior to receiver）

私は先生に手紙をいただきました。
わたし　せんせい　　てがみ
I received a letter from my teacher.

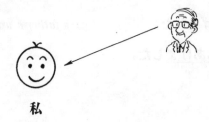

私

For receiving from family, only **もらう** can be used:

○　私は父にお金をもらいました。　　*I received money from father.*
　　ちち　かね

×　私は父にお金をいただきました。

3. The くれる *(give ingroup)* type

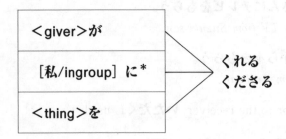

→鈴木さんが私にテレビをくれる。
　すずき
Suzuki-san gives me a TV.

→アニルさんが弟に本をくれる。
　　　　　　　おとうと　ほん
Anil-san gives my younger brother a book.

When the giver is superior to the speaker, or a member of the speaker's group, **くださる** is used:

> ### くれる （giver is equal/inferior to receiver）

田中さんが（私に）*手紙をくれました。
たなか　　　わたし　　　てがみ
Tanaka-san gave me a letter.

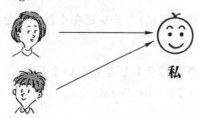

> ### くださる （giver is superior to receiver）

1. **先生は（私に）*手紙をくださいました。**
せんせい
   My teacher gave me a letter.

2. **先生が 弟 に本をくださいました。**
おとうと　ほん
   My teacher gave my younger brother a book.

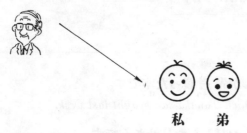

私　　弟

くださる conjugates in a special way as follows:
くださらない，くださいます，くださって，くださった，くださらなかった

In **くれる** type sentences, the giver （＝ subject） must be an outgroup person （including the listener）, and the receiver must be the speaker **私** or a member of his group （e.g. a family member）.

However, you should use **くれる** sentences when the giver is a member of your family.

1. **父が（私に）*お金をくれました。** *Father gave me money.*
ちち　　　　　かね

2. **弟が（私に）*CD をくれます。**　*My younger brother will give me a CD.*

GN

Don't use **くださる** when referring to family members.

⚠ **私に** can only be used in the **くれる** *(give ingroup)* type, NEVER with the **もらう** or **あげる** types; therefore the following are incorrect:

1. × リサ：鈴木さんは私にテレビをあげました。
   <ruby>鈴木<rt>すずき</rt></ruby>

   ○ リサ：鈴木さんは（私に）＊テレビをくれました。
   Suzuki-san gave me a TV.

   or ○ リサ：私は鈴木さんにテレビをもらいました。
   I received a TV from Suzuki-san.

2. × 鈴木：リサさんは私にテレビをもらいました。

   ○ 鈴木：私はリサさんにテレビをあげました。
   I gave Lisa-san a TV.

＊Because the identity of the receiver is obvious, **私に** is often omitted in **く れる** sentences.

Ⅲ. Noun modification ⟨2⟩

Examples

① これは、田中さんが先週買った本です。
   <ruby>田中<rt>たなか</rt></ruby> <ruby>先週<rt>せんしゅう</rt></ruby> <ruby>買<rt>か</rt></ruby> <ruby>本<rt>ほん</rt></ruby>
   This is the book which Tanaka-san bought last week.

② こちらは、きのうお話ししたリサさんです。
   <ruby>話<rt>はな</rt></ruby>
   This is Lisa-san whom I talked about yesterday.

③ アニルさんの作る料理はおいしいです。
   <ruby>作<rt>つく</rt></ruby> <ruby>料理<rt>りょうり</rt></ruby>
   The food which Anil-san cooks is delicious.

【*Explanation*】

1. Verbs modifying nouns
We have seen how to modify nouns with other nouns, **-i** adjectives, and **na** adjectives: ⇨L10GN I

日本語の　本　　　　*a Japanese book*
にほんご　ほん

新しい　本　　　　*a new book*
あたら

きれいな　本　　　　*a beautiful book*

Verbs, or sentences ending in verbs, can also modify a noun:

私がきのう買った　本　　　*a book which I bought yesterday*
わたし　　　か

Two general rules apply:

1 ） The modifying section precedes the noun it modifies, as always in Japanese.

2 ） The predicate (verb etc.) before the noun is in the plain form.

Let's see now how 人 *a person* can be modified:
ひと

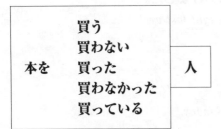

買う　　　　　　　*a/the person who (will) buy a book*
買わない　　　　　*a/the person who doesn't buy a book*
本を　買った　　人　*a/the person who bought a book*
買わなかった　　　*a/the person who didn't buy a book*
買っている　　　　*a/the person who is buying a book*

Nouns can also be modified in various other ways:

きのう田中さんがデパートで本を買いました。
たなか

Tanaka-san bought a book at the department store yesterday.

↓ modifying 本 *a book*

［きのう田中さんがデパートで買った］本

a book which Tanaka-san bought at the department store yesterday

↓ modifying デパート *a department store*

［きのう田中さんが本を買った］デパート

the department store where Tanaka-san bought a book yesterday

↓ modifying 田中さん *Tanaka-san*

［きのうデパートで本を買った］田中さん

Tanaka-san, who bought a book at the department store yesterday

GN

Modifier ＋[N] functions in the same way as [N], so it can appear in various positions in a sentence.

１）Modifier ＋[N] as a subject

1. <u>きのう本を買った人</u>はだれですか。
Who is the person that bought a book yesterday?

2. <u>先週買った本</u>はおもしろいです。
The book I bought last week is interesting.

２）Modifier ＋[N] as an object

3. <u>あそこで本を買っている人</u>を知っていますか。
Do you know the person who is buying a book over there?

4. 私は<u>先週買った本</u>をリサさんにあげました。
I gave Lisa-san the book which I bought last week.

３）Modifier ＋[N] as a predicate

5. これは、<u>日曜日に買った本</u>です。
This is a book which I bought on Sunday.

Various types of noun modification（which correspond to relative clauses in English）are illustrated below; modifying sections are given in ［ ］:

6. ［私が買いたい］本はこれです。
The book which I want to buy is this one.
買いたい： [V(base)] たい ⇨L7GN I

7. ［電気がついている］部屋はアニルさんの部屋です。
The room with the light on is Anil-san's room.
ついている： [V-te] いる ⇨L8GN V

8. ［まだ習っていない］漢字がたくさんあります。
There are (still) a lot of Kanji which I haven't learnt yet.
習っていない： [V-te] いない ⇨L8GN VI

2. が／の for the subject of a modifying clause

The subject within a modifying section is normally indicated by **が**, not by **は**, **の** sometimes replaces **が** when the modifying clause is relatively short.

1. ［きのう田中さんがデパートで買った］本を見せてください。
   Show me the book which Tanaka-san bought at the department store yesterday.

2. ［田中さん　の／が　作った］料理　はおいしかった。
   The food which Tanaka-san cooked was delicious.

3. アニルさんは［せ　の／が　高い］人　です。
   Anil-san is a tall person. (lit. Anil-san is a person who is tall.)

Ⅳ. 〜ている〈2〉: *be V-ing*: progressive action

Examples

① アニルさんはいま手紙を書いています。　*Anil-san is writing a letter.*

② きのう一日中雨が降っていました。　*It was raining all day yesterday.*

【Explanation】

[V-te] いる expresses progressive action that still continues at the present (refer to Lesson 5 GN Ⅱ on how to form the -te form).

[V-te] いた expresses an action／state which continued for a period of time in the past (②):

1. 子どものとき、インドに住んでいました。
   I lived in India when I was a child.

2. きのうの午後 5 時から 7 時まで黒い車が止まっていました。
   A black car was parked (there/here) from 5 till 7 yesterday afternoon.

[V-te] いる／います is often contracted as [V-te] る／ます in informal Japanese:

1. A : 何をして（い）るんですか。
   What are you doing?

   B : 国の友だちに手紙を書いて（い）ます。
   I'm writing a letter to a friend back home.

2. 田中さんがそう言って（い）ました。
   Tanaka-san said/was saying so.

143

V. ～ばかりだ: *(only) just ～*

Examples

① 鈴木さんはテレビを買ったばかりです。
Suzuki-san just bought a TV.

② 先月日本に来たばかりです。
I only just came to Japan last month.

【*Explanation*】

[V-ta] ばかりだ indicates that the action [V-ta] took place only recently.

[V-ta] ばかりなので／ばかりで is used to indicate that a situation obtains because the action [V-ta] took place only recently:

1. 日本へ来たばかりなので、日本語がよくわかりません。
   I've only just come to Japan, so I don't understand Japanese well.

2. 日本語の勉強を始めたばかりで、まだよくわかりません。
   I've only just started to learn Japanese, and don't understand it well yet.

VI. 〈quantity/duration〉＋も: *as many/long as*

Example

① きのうは１０時間も勉強しました。
Yesterday I studied as long as 10 hours.

【*Explanation*】

The difference to きのうは１０時間勉強しました is that ① emphasizes that 10 hours is an unduly long time. Compare the sentence pairs below:

1. **アニルさんはアイスクリームを３つ食べました。**
   た

   Anil-san ate three ice creams.

   アニルさんはアイスクリームを３つも食べました。

   Anil-san ate THREE ICE CREAMS!

   (＝Anil-san ate as many as three ice creams.)

2. **田中さんのアパートにはテレビが３台あります。**
   たなか　　　　　　　　　　　　　　　　　だい

   Tanaka-san has three TVs in her apartment.

   田中さんのアパートにはテレビが３台もあります。

   Tanaka-san has THREE TVs in her apartment.

   (＝Tanaka-san has as many as three TVs.)　　　　⇨L12GNⅨ

GN

145

Conversation Notes

\<General Information\>

1. Introductions —3

When you are introduced to someone you have heard about from others, you can mention it as follows:

① A：Cさん。こちら、この間お話ししたBさん。

　　B：Bです。よろしくお願いします。

　　C：こちらこそ。Cです。

おうわさ お名前	は＜someone＞から	いつも よく	聞いています。

I	always often	hear	about you your name	from ＜someone＞

2. Building a relationship in a conversation

We saw that a variety of expressions is available for starting a conversation. However, you also need to know how to keep it going. When talking to a good friend, no fixed rules apply, but when speaking to a stranger or a **Higher**, a fixed pattern generally applies:

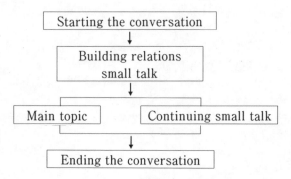

146

Before getting down to the main topic, question/answer or compliment/response exchanges generally take place; typical topics include the following:

The weather（天気）
Your country and family（国や家族）
Japanese life（日本の生活）
Your research and work（研究や仕事／勉強）
Your Japanese（日本語）

These exchanges are used to establish a relationship between speaker and listener, not to gain information or satisfy people's curiosity. When you speak Japanese, the Japanese will often say「日本語、お上手ですね。」, even if your Japanese is rather basic. Although you can respond to this compliment by saying「どうもありがとうございます。」if you think you're quite good, etiquette demands that you are modest about it, replying with「いいえ、そんなことありませんよ。」or「いいえ、まだまだですよ。」
⇨L13CN S-3

① A：日本語は、難しいでしょう。↗
Japanese language is difficult, isn't it?

B：ええ。そうですね。漢字が難しいですね。
Yes, Kanji are difficult.

② A：漢字も読めるんですか。すごいですね。
You can also read Kanji? That's very impressive!

B：そんなことないですよ。
Not really.

③ A：日本語、お上手ですね。
You speak Japanese really well.

B：｜ありがとうございます。
｜いいえ。そんなことないですよ。
｜Thank you.
｜No, not really.

④ A：どのくらい日本語を勉強しているんですか。
How long have you been studying Japanese?

B：まだ、3か月しか勉強していないんです。
I've only been studying Japanese for 3 months.

<Strategies>

S-1. How to apologize and give an excuse

a. Apologizing

For apologizing, the following expressions are useful:

<reason>て、	ごめん（なさい）。☺
	すみません。🔲
	申しわけありません。🔲
	申しわけございません。🔲

As **ごめんなさい** and **ごめん** are rather casual, do not use them to a **Higher**. When you apologize for what has already been done, use past-tense forms.

① 学生：宿題をわすれて、すみません。
I'm sorry I forgot my homework.

先生：いいえ。じゃ、あした出してくださいね。
That's all right. Hand it in tomorrow.

② 学生：きのうはクラスを欠席して、申しわけありませんでした。
Sorry I missed yesterday's class.

先生：熱があったんですって。↗ だいじょうぶですか。
I heard you had a fever. Are you all right?

b. Giving an excuse

It is common to attach an excuse to your apology; this is done with < reason > **もんですから** *because* < reason >:

① お話がわからなくて、すみません。まだ日本へ来て１か月なもんですから。
I'm sorry. I can't understand what you said because I have been in Japan only two months.

② 授業を休んで、申しわけありませんでした。熱があったもんですから。
I'm sorry I couldn't come to the class because I had a fever.

③ 遅くなっちゃってごめん。道がこんでたもんだから。
Sorry I'm late. (It's because) I got caught in the traffic.

148

You can include reason and apology in one sentence by using **もんですから／ものですから** or **ので**（but not just **から**）. {S₁} **から**、{S₂}, implies that {S₁} is not given as an explanation（of your personal circumstances）but as a logical cause for {S₂}, which would be inappropriate.

| {S₁} | ものですから
ので | {S₂} |

① すみません。子どもが病気だった ｜ ものですから、
ので
×から ｜ 欠席しました。

I didn't come to the class because my child was sick.

② 今ちょっと忙しい ｜ もんですから、
ので
×から ｜ お手伝いできません。

I cannot help you at the moment because I'm busy.

An apology/excuse is often given in stages:

③ A：きのう、欠席してすみませんでした。

I am sorry I was absent yesterday.

B：いや、かまわないよ。🎓

Oh, never mind.

A：実は、子供が病気だった ｜ もんですから。
ので。

Actually, my child was ill.

④ A：手伝うことが、できなくてすみません。

I'm sorry I can't help you.

B：いえ、いいんですよ。

Oh, never mind.

A：いま、ちょっと忙しい ｜ ので。
ものですから。

You see, I'm rather busy at the moment.

CN

149

S-2. How to confirm what you heard from someone

To confirm a rumour, you can use **〜んだって**, with rising intonation.

〈rumour〉	んだって。↗ 🙂	*I heard that 〜, - is it true?*
	んですって。↗ 😐	
	と聞きましたが。😐	

① A：リサイクルの安い店<small>やす みせ</small>さがしてるんだって。↗ 🙂

    B：ええ。

② A：田中<small>たなか</small>さん、来月結婚<small>らいげつけっこん</small>するんですって。↗ 😐

    B：そうなんです。

③ A：山下<small>やました</small>さんのともだちが病気<small>びょうき</small>なんだって。↗ 🙂

    B：そう。↘

Used with a falling intonation, it means *I hear/understand that 〜*.

リサさんはリサイクルの安い店をさがしてるんだって。↘ 🙂

This expression can't be used to a **Higher**.

× A：先生、来週漢字<small>せんせい らいしゅうかんじ</small>の試験<small>しけん</small>があるんだって。↗

○ B：先生、来週漢字の試験がある | と聞きましたが。<small>き</small>
　　　　　　　　　　　　　　　 | そうですが。

I heard that we'll have a kanji test next week, sir.

S-3. How to bring up the main topic

After some preliminary topics (about the weather, work/study, or a current topic), you can come to your main topic. We've already come across some expressions, such as **じゃ**, **実は**<small>じつ</small> and **で** that are useful for steering a conversation; here, let us look at **ところで**, which can be used to change the topic of a conversation:

The first topic

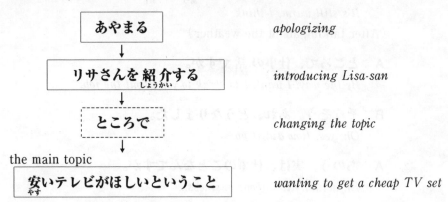

あやまる	*apologizing*
リサさんを紹介する _{しょうかい}	*introducing Lisa-san*
ところで	*changing the topic*

the main topic

安いテレビがほしいということ _{やす}	*wanting to get a cheap TV set*

In the above conversation, Suzuki-san first apologized to Lisa-san and Tanaka-san (first topic), and Tanaka-san introduced Lisa-san to Suzuki-san (second topic); after that, Tanaka-san took control and changed the line of conversation by introducing a new topic.

You can shorten the preliminary topics with **さっそくなんですが** (*May I come straight to the point?*):

　　A：きょうは寒いですね。
　　　　　_{さむ}

　　B：ええ、本当に。
　　　　　　_{ほんとう}

　　A：さっそくなんですが。

　　B：ええ。

　　A：この間お話ししたアルバイトのことなんですが。
　　　　　_{あいだ}　_{はな}

When the main topic isn't clear to the hearer, the speaker will often feel the need to introduce it by using **ところで** or **実は**.
　　　　　　　　　　　　　　　　　　　　　　_{じつ}

ところで、 実は _{じつ}	～の	こと 話 _{はなし}	なんですが。

① 　A：寒くなりましたね。
　　　　It's cold, isn't it.

　　B：ええ、ほんとうに。
　　　　Yes, that's true.

　　A：お国では、今ごろはいかがですか。
　　　　_{くに}　　_{いま}
　　　　How about your country at the moment?

CN

151

B：そうですね。まだちょっと暑いと思いますけど。

It's still warm, I think.

（After talking about the weather）

A：ところで、仕事の話ですが。

By the way, I wanted to speak to you about the job.

B：そうそう。あれ、どうなりました。

Oh, yes. How did it go?

② **A**：あのう、実は、仕事のことなんですが。

Er, actually it's about business...

B：仕事のこと。↗

Business?

A：ええ。……（continued）

Yes...

S-4. How to make and accept an offer

The following expressions are useful for making an offer:

[V-te] もいい。　　　　　　　*I can ～ for/to you.*

[V-te] あげてもいい。

[V-base] ましょうか。　　　　*Shall/can I ～ for you?*

[V-te] あげましょうか。

① ぼく、新しいのを買ったばかりだから、古いのをあげてもいいよ。

I've just bought a new one so I can give you the other one/old one if you like.

② 重いから、運んであげましょうか。

That's heavy. Do you want me to give you a hand.

③ 重いから、私が運んであげましょうか。

That's heavy. Can I carry it for you?

That's heavy. I can carry it for you if you like.

④ じゃあ、持ってきてあげましょうか。

I can take it for you if you like.

This use of ［V-te］**もいい** and ［V-te］**あげる** is inappropriate to a senior; instead, you can use an expression of request or intention:

① **どうぞ古いのを使ってください。**　　*Please use the old one.*

② **重いですから、運びましょう。**　　*That's heavy. I'll carry it (for you).*

③ **私が持ってきますから。**　　*I'll bring it(, so don't worry).*

Before you accept an offer, make sure to confirm that it is really all right 「**でも、よろしいんですか。／いいんですか。／いいの。**↗（*Is it all right/Are you sure?*）」; if the answer is yes, you can accept with 「**じゃ、えんりょなく。**」 and/or an expression of gratitude:

① A：**じゃ、私がなおしてあげましょう。**　　*I'll repair it for you.*

B：**えっ、でも、いいんですか。**

A：**ええ、もちろんかまいませんよ。**

B：**そうですか。どうもありがとうございます。**

② A：**どうぞこれ、使ってください。**　　*Please use this.*

B：**えっ、でも、よろしいんですか。**

A：**ええ。どうぞ、どうぞ。**

B：**じゃ、えんりょなく。どうもありがとうございます。**

When you don't want to accept the offer, you can use 「**けっこうです。**(*No, thank you.*)」. However, you must be very careful not to offend the other person:

A：**どうぞ、これ、使ってください。**

B：**あ、いえ。そんな、けっこうです。**　　*I can't accept that...*

A：**かまいませんから、どうぞ。**

B：**いえ、ほんとうにけっこうですから。**　　*Thank you very much but it's all right.*

A：**そうですか。**

To people who hesitate to accept, 「**どうぞ、ごえんりょなく。**(*Please don't hesitate to accept my offer.*)」 can be used:

A：じゃ、私がやってあげましょう。　*I'll do it for you.*

B：えっ、でも。

A：今、時間がありますから。

B：でも、ほんとうによろしいんですか。

A：ええ。どうぞ、ごえんりょなく。

B：すみません。じゃ、お願いします。

S-5. How to express modesty

Have you ever been at the receiving end of the following conversation?

日本人：日本語お上手ですね。

外国人：そんな。

日本人：どのくらい、日本語を勉強しているんですか。

外国人：2か月くらいです。

日本人：えっ。2か月ですか。すごいですね。

Japanese meeting foreigners who speak good (or not so good!) Japanese often express surprise and praise; it is advisable to react with **いいえ** rather than **どうもありがとうございます**, even if you speak Japanese well:

① 日本人：日本語お上手ですね。

　外国人：いいえ。そんなこと（ないですよ）。　*Oh, not really.*

② 日本人：日本語お上手ですね。

　外国人：いいえ。それほどでも（ないですよ）。*No, I'm not that good.*

③ 日本人：日本語お上手ですね。

　外国人：いいえ。まだ……（上手じゃないですよ）。
　　　　　No, I'm still (quite hopeless).

④ 日本人：日本語お上手ですね。

　外国人：いいえ。とんでもありません。　　*No, not at all!*

第14課

忘れ物の問い合わせ
わす　もの　　と　あ
Enquiring about a lost article

OBJECTIVES:

GRAMMAR

Ⅰ. Potential verbs

Ⅱ. あげる／さしあげる
　　～てもらう／いただく: giving and receiving〈2〉
　　くれる／くださる

Ⅲ. ～に行く／来る（に〈6〉）: *going/coming for the*
　　　　　　　　　　　　　　　　　　purpose of～

Ⅳ. 〈time〉までに vs 〈time〉まで

CONVERSATION

＜General Information＞
1. The lost-property office
2. Shape, colour and size

＜Strategies＞
S-1. How to enquire about something you left
　　　behind
S-2. How to answer questions
S-3. How to confirm information —3.
S-4. How to describe something
S-5. How to express one's feelings.

Model Conversation

Characters : Tanaka（田中）, staff members A（職員 A） and B（職員 B） of a bus company

Situation : Tanaka-san left behind a brown paper bag on the bus from the station to the university. In the bag there was a book she borrowed from a friend, so she rings up the Joso bus office to enquire about it.

Flow-chart :

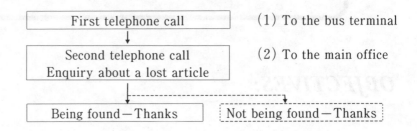

（1）―電話1 （バス・ターミナル）―

田　中：もしもし、常総バスのターミナルですか。
職員A：はい。
田　中：あの、バスの中に忘れ物をしたんですが。
職員A：ええとね。忘れ物はここじゃないんですよ。
田　中：あ、そうなんですか。
職員A：駅前の営業所であつかってるんですよ。
田　中：そうですか。すみません、電話番号、教えていただけますか。
職員A：はい。いいですか。
田　中：はい。
職員A：７４の……
田　中：はい。
職員A：５９４６です。
田　中：どうも。

（2）―電話2 （駅前の営業所）―

田　中：あの、常総バスの営業所ですか。
職員B：はい。
田　中：けさ、バスの中に袋を忘れちゃったんですが。

職員Ｂ：どこ行き。
田　中：大学正門行きです。
職員Ｂ：何時ごろ。
田　中：ええと、8時40分ごろ大学の正門に着いたんですが。
職員Ｂ：あ、そう。で、どんな袋。
田　中：茶色の紙袋です。中に本が入ってるんですけど。
職員Ｂ：茶の紙袋ね。
田　中：ええ。
職員Ｂ：ちょっと待って。
田　中：はい。

＊　　　＊　　　＊

職員Ｂ：もしもし。
田　中：はい。
職員Ｂ：届いてますよ。茶色の紙袋ね。
田　中：あ、そうですか。本、入ってますか。
職員Ｂ：本ね。あ、ありますよ。
田　中：ああ、よかった。
職員Ｂ：それで、きょう、取りに来られますか。
田　中：ええ。夕方になると思いますが。
職員Ｂ：じゃ、5時までに来てください。
田　中：はい、わかりました。ありがとうございます。

Report

　田中さんはバスの中に本が入っている茶色の紙袋を忘れました。それで、まずバス・ターミナルに電話をかけて、忘れ物の問い合わせをしました。すると職員は、忘れ物は駅前の営業所であつかっていると答えました。

　次に、駅前の営業所に電話をかけました。営業所の職員は忘れ物をした場所、時間、色や形などについていろいろ質問しました。そして、紙袋が見つかったので、田中さんは夕方取りに行きました。

MC

New Words and Expressions

Words in the conversation

職員	しょくいん	employee
ターミナル		(bus) terminal
もしもし		Hello
常総バス	じょうそうバス	Joso Bus (company)
忘れ物	わすれもの	lost article
駅前	えきまえ	area near the station
営業所	えいぎょうしょ	office
あつかう		to deal with
袋	ふくろ	bag
忘れる	わすれる	to forget
正門	せいもん	the main entrance/gate
着く	つく	to arrive, to reach
茶色	ちゃいろ	brown
紙袋	かみぶくろ	paper bag
茶	ちゃ	shortened form of 茶色
届く	とどく	arrive c.f. 届ける
取る	とる	to get, to take
～までに		by ～（time）

＜Expressions in the conversation＞

もしもし、   *Hello (on the telephone)* ⇨L7CN S-2

ええとね。   *Let's see...*
ええと⇨まとめ1BⅡ3-c

～であつかってるんですよ。   *(We) are holding it at ～.*
あつかってる＝あつかっている ⇨L8GNV

電話番号、教えていただけますか。   *Can you give me the phone number, please?*
でんわばんごう おし
いただけます is the potential form（⇨GNⅠ）of いただきます.
cf. ［V-te］いただく ⇨GNⅡ, CN S-1b

いいですか。   *Are you ready?*

158

バスの中に 袋を忘れちゃったんですが。　　*I left a bag behind on the bus.* ⇨CN S-1
忘れちゃった is a casual contraction of 忘れてしまった.
cf. [V-te] しまう shows that an action takes place in spite of the speaker's intention. ⇨L22GN Ⅱ

ああ、よかった。　　　　　　　　　　　*Oh, thank Heavens!*

取りに来られますか。　　　　　　　　*Can you come and get it?*
　　　〜に来る ⇨GN Ⅲ

Words in the report

まず		*first of all*
問い合わせ	といあわせ	*inquiry*
すると、		*and, then*
次に、	つぎに	*next,*
答える	こたえる	*to answer*
〜について		*about 〜*
質問する	しつもんする	*to ask a question*

MC

Grammar Notes

Ⅰ. Potential verbs

Examples

① 私は日本語が話せます。
わたし　にほんご　はな
I can speak Japanese.

② 日本人の名前がおぼえられません。
にほんじん　なまえ
I can't remember Japanese names.

③ 図書館で本が借りられます。
としょかん　ほん　か
One/you can borrow books from/at the library.

④ この水は飲めませんよ。
みず　の
This water is not drinkable. (＝You can't drink this water.)

【*Explanation*】

1. Meaning of potential sentences

A potential sentence expresses
(1) what the subject can do (①②)
(2) what is possible (③④)

Examples ① and ② refer to the subject's ability of speaking Japanese and remembering Japanese names, whereas ③ and ④ are concerned with the possibility of borrowing books and drinking the water.

2. Structure of potential sentences

Potential verbs take the following structure.

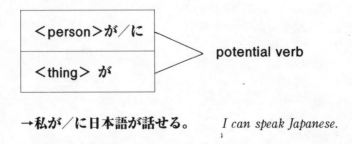

→私が／に日本語が話せる。　　*I can speak Japanese.*

Note that the object of a potential verb is marked by **が** rather than **を**.

私 は日本語を話す。　　　　*I speak Japanese.*
わたし　にほんご　　はな
↓
私 は日本語が話せる。　　　*I can speak Japanese.*

---

1. リサさんは漢字が書けます。　　*Lisa-san can write Kanji.*
　　　　　　かんじ　か

2. 日本の歌が歌えます。　　　　　*I can sing a Japanese song.*
　　うた　うた

3. A：どのくらい泳げますか。　　*How far can you swim?*
　　　　　　およ
　 B：1000メートルぐらい泳げます。　*I can swim 1000 meters or so.*

For contrast/emphasis, ＜person＞**には** is sometimes used:

4. A：日本語でスピーチしてください。　*Please give a speech in Japanese.*
　 B：いや、私にはできません。　　　*Goodness. No, I can't/couldn't.*

GN

Potential verbs				
Ordinary verbs	Non-past pos.	Non-past neg.	Past pos.	Past neg.
Group Ⅰ	-u → -eru			
kaku *to write* 書く	kakeru 書ける	kakenai 書けない	kaketa 書けた	kakenakatta 書けなかった
hanasu *to speak* 話す	hanaseru 話せる	hanasenai 話せない	hanaseta 話せた	hanasenakatta 話せなかった
motsu *to carry* 持つ	moteru 持てる	motenai 持てない	moteta 持てた	motenakatta 持てなかった
Group Ⅱ	-ru → -rareru			
taberu *to eat* 食べる	taberareru 食べられる	taberarenai 食べられない	taberareta 食べられた	taberarenakatta 食べられなかった
miru *to see* 見る	mirareru 見られる	mirarenai 見られない	mirareta 見られた	mirarenakatta 見られなかった

Ordinary verbs		Non-past pos.	Non-past neg.	Past pos.	Past neg.
Group Ⅲ					
kuru 来る	*to come*	korareru 来られる	korarenai 来られない	korareta 来られた	korarenakatta 来られなかった
suru する	*to do*	dekiru できる	dekinai できない	dekita できた	dekinakatta できなかった

The following are sometimes heard in spoken Japanese.

(1) Group Ⅱ

見れる　（←見られる）　　　　食べれる　（←食べられる）

(2) Group Ⅲ

来れる　（←来られる）

(3) Group Ⅰ

行かれる（←行ける）

3. Potential verbs and controllability

Potential verbs can be formed only from verbs whose actions can be controlled by the actor; therefore verbs whose actions cannot be controlled by the actor, such as **ある** *to exist/have,* **開く** *to open,* **閉まる** *to close,* **決まる** *to be decided* do not have potential forms:

〇　ドアが開きます。　　　　　*The door opens.*

✕　ドアが開かれます。

Although potential verbs are originally formed from verbs whose actions can be controlled, the resulting potential verbs cannot be controlled. **見える**, **聞こえる**（⇨ L12GNⅦ）, **できる** *can* (this Lesson) and **わかる** *to understand* are also potential verbs.

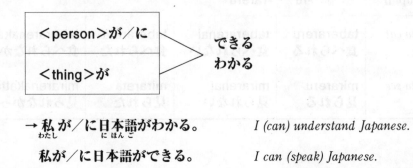

→私が／に日本語がわかる。　　　*I (can) understand Japanese.*

私が／に日本語ができる。　　　*I can (speak) Japanese.*

1. 私は日本語が少しわかります。　*I understand Japanese a little.*
   （わたし）（すこ）

2. 田中さんはダンスができます。　*Tanaka-san can dance.*
   （た なか）

II.　あげる／さしあげる
〜て　もらう／いただく　: giving and receiving 〈2〉
　　くれる／くださる

Examples

① （私は）リサさんの仕事を手伝ってあげました。
　　　　　　　　　（しごと）（てつだ）
I helped Lisa-san with her work.
(lit. I did Lisa-san the favour of helping her work.)

② 私はアニルさんに仕事を手伝ってもらいました。
I got Anil-san to help me with my work.
(lit. I received the favour from Anil-san of helping me with my work.)

③ アニルさんが（私の）仕事を手伝ってくれました。
Anil-san helped me with my work.
(lit. Anil-san (kindly) did me the favour of helping me with my work.)

GN

【*Explanation*】

In Japanese, not only things but also actions can be given and received. When verbs of giving and receiving are attached to the **-te** form of a verb, the implication is that someone does the action of the verb for someone else's benefit.

The relationship between ＜giver＞ and ＜receiver＞ with [V-te] あげる, [V-te] もらう and [V-te] くれる are the same as with あげる, もらう and くれる (⇨ L13GNII), the ＜giver＞ corresponds to the person doing a favour and the ＜receiver＞ to the person receiving a favour:

1. The あげる *(give outgroup)* type

　1. 鈴木さんがリサさんに漢字を教えてあげました。
　　　（すずき）　　　　　（かんじ）（おし）
　Suzuki-san taught Lisa-san Kanji.
　(lit. Suzuki-san did Lisa-san the favour of teaching her Kanji.)

2. 私は鈴木さんの仕事を手伝ってあげました。
わたし すずき しごと てつだ

I helped Suzuki-san with his work.

(lit. I did Suzuki-san the favour of helping him with his work.)

When understood from the context, the receiver can be omitted:

3. リサさんがさいふを落としたので、いっしょに警察に行ってあげました。
お けいさつ い

As Lisa-san had lost her purse, I went to the police station with her.

(lit. As Lisa-san had lost her purse, I did her the favour of going to the police station with her.)

As with the **あげる** type, **〜てやる** can be used for doing a favour to younger members of family/animals etc.

4. 私は弟の部屋をそうじしてやりました。
おとうと へや

I cleaned my brother's room for him.

(lit. I did my brother the favour of cleaning his room.)

Note that **〜てあげる** needs to be used with care as it explicitly expresses the idea that the giver is doing the receiver a favour; for this reason it is often better to use a verb without **〜てあげる**:

(more appropriate) **手伝いましょうか。**   *Shall I help you?*

(less appropriate) **手伝ってあげましょうか。**

2. The もらう *(receive)* type

1. リサさんは鈴木さんに日本語を教えてもらいます。
にほんご

Lisa-san has Suzuki-san teach her Japanese.

(lit. Lisa-san receives the favour from Suzuki-san of teaching her Japanese.)

2. 私は田中さんに仕事を手伝ってもらいました。
たなか

I got Tanaka-san to help me with my work.

(lit. I received the favour from Tanaka-san of helping me with my work.)

3. 私は姉に部屋をそうじしてもらった。
あね

I had my sister clean my room for me.

(lit. I received the favour from my sister of cleaning my room.)

4. リサさんはさいふを落<ruby>落<rt>お</rt></ruby>としたので、田中<ruby>田中<rt>た なか</rt></ruby>さんにいっしょに警察<ruby>警察<rt>けいさつ</rt></ruby>に行<ruby>行<rt>い</rt></ruby>ってもらいました。

Lisa-san had Tanaka-san go to the police station with her because she had lost her purse.

(lit. As Lisa-san had lost her purse, she received from Tanaka-san the favour of going to the police station with her.)

With 〜てもらう sentences (especially with future actions), the implication often is that the subject (who often is the speaker) is getting the performer to do the favour by asking or persuading him/her:

5. 手紙<ruby>手紙<rt>て がみ</rt></ruby>は日本人<ruby>日本人<rt>に ほんじん</rt></ruby>の友<ruby>友<rt>とも</rt></ruby>だちに書<ruby>書<rt>か</rt></ruby>いてもらいます。

I'll get a Japanese friend to write a letter (for me).

6. 父<ruby>父<rt>ちち</rt></ruby>にランボルギーニを買<ruby>買<rt>か</rt></ruby>ってもらいます。

I'll get father to buy me a Lamborghini.

3. The くれる *give ingroup* type

1. 鈴木<ruby>鈴木<rt>す ずき</rt></ruby>さんが漢字<ruby>漢字<rt>かん じ</rt></ruby>を教<ruby>教<rt>おし</rt></ruby>えてくれました。

Suzuki-san was kind enough to teach me Kanji.

2. 鈴木<ruby>鈴木<rt>す ずき</rt></ruby>さんが仕事<ruby>仕事<rt>し ごと</rt></ruby>を手伝<ruby>手伝<rt>て つだ</rt></ruby>ってくれました。

Suzuki-san was kind enough to help me with my work.

3. 田中さんが弟<ruby>弟<rt>おとうと</rt></ruby>の部屋<ruby>部屋<rt>へ や</rt></ruby>をそうじしてくれました。

Tanaka-san cleaned my brother's room for him.

4. さいふを落としたので、山田<ruby>山田<rt>やま だ</rt></ruby>さんがいっしょに警察に行ってくださいました。

As I lost my purse, Yamada-san kindly went to the police station with me.

Ⅲ. 〜に行く／来<ruby>来<rt>く</rt></ruby>る（にく6）: *going/coming for the purpose of 〜*

Examples

① 東京<ruby>東京<rt>とうきょう</rt></ruby>へ買物<ruby>買物<rt>かいもの</rt></ruby>に行きます。　　*I'll go to Tokyo to shop.*

② 図書館<ruby>図書館<rt>と しょかん</rt></ruby>へ本<ruby>本<rt>ほん</rt></ruby>を読<ruby>読<rt>よ</rt></ruby>みに行きます。　*I'll go to the library to read (books).*

③ 日本<ruby>日本<rt>に ほん</rt></ruby>に経済<ruby>経済<rt>けいざい</rt></ruby>を勉強<ruby>勉強<rt>べんきょう</rt></ruby>しに来<ruby>来<rt>き</rt></ruby>ました。　*I came to Japan to study economics.*

GN

【*Explanation*】

Verbs of coming and going can be used with an indication of the purpose (marked by に) for which the action is carried out:

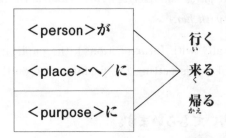

→ 私が東京へ買物に行く。　　　　　　　*I go to Tokyo to shop.*

Like in the case of ordinary nouns, に can also be attached to verbal nouns that express an activity (ex. 買物 *shopping*, 勉強 *studying*, スキー *skiing*) (①); compare B's sentence below with ③:

A：日本に何をしにいらっしゃいましたか。
What did you come to Japan for?

B：経済の勉強に来ました。
I came to study economics. (lit. I came here for the study of economics.)

に can also be attached to a verb base (②):

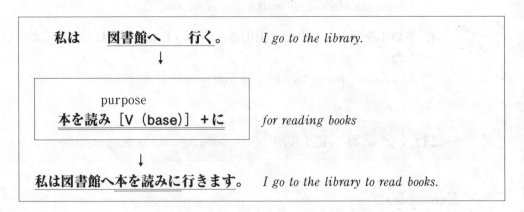

Note that ＜place＞へ／に is required rather than ＜place＞で, even though ＜place＞ is a place of action; this is due to the verbs of motion (coming/going).

IV. 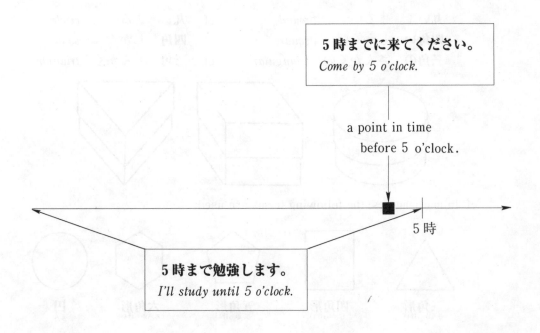 ＜time＞までに vs ＜time＞まで

＜time＞までに indicates that the action is completed no later than the time given:

1. 5時までに来てください。　　　　*Come by 5 o'clock.*

2. 8時半までに行きます。　　　　*I'll be there by 8:30.*

3. あしたまでにおぼえます。　　　　*I'll memorize it by tomorrow.*

＜time＞まで, on the other hand, indicates that the action continues until the time given: ⇨L7GNIV

4. 5時まで勉強します。
I'll study until 5.

5. A：まだ* ここにいらっしゃるんですか。
Are you still staying here?

　　B：ええ、あしたまでここにいます。
Yes, I'll stay here until tomorrow.

***まだ** used in positive sentences, means *still*.

The difference between **までに** and **まで** can be illustrated as follows.

```
                              ┌─────────────────────────┐
                              │ 5時までに来てください。  │
                              │ Come by 5 o'clock.       │
                              └─────────────────────────┘
                                          │
                                          ▼
                                   a point in time
                                   before 5 o'clock.
                                          │
                                          ▼
   ◄──────────────────────────────────■──┼──────────►
                                          5時
                      ┌─────────────────────┐
                      │ 5時まで勉強します。  │
                      │ I'll study until 5 o'clock. │
                      └─────────────────────┘
```

Conversation Notes

<General Information>

1. The lost-property office

If you left something behind on a bus or a train, you can make inquiries at the bus company or at the station office; lost articles are normally kept in the terminal station's 遺失物係 (**いしつぶつがかり**, *lost-property office*). If you lost something in a department store, a restaurant or a hotel, call the main office. When you are unsure where you lost something, the section in charge at the 警察 (**けいさつ**, *police station*) may be able to help.

When you enquire about a lost article, you may be asked for information about when and where you lost it and what it looks like (colour, shape, size, contents). At the office you will have to give your personal details to reclaim the lost article.

2. Shape, colour and size

a. Shape (形, かたち):

丸い	まるい	*round*	cf.	丸	まる	*circle*
四角い	しかくい	*square*	cf.	四角	しかく	*square*
三角の	さんかくの	*triangular*	cf.	三角	さんかく	*triangle*

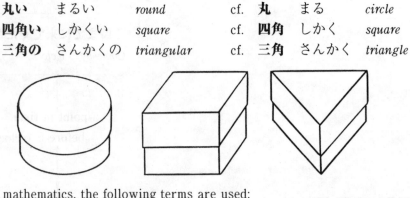

cf. In mathematics, the following terms are used:

三角形　　　　四角形　　　　五角形　　　　六角形　　　　円
さんかっけい　しかっけい　　ごかっけい　　ろっかっけい　えん

168

箱	はこ	box
袋	ふくろ	bag, sack
かばん		bag, suitcase
つつみ		package
ふうとう		envelope

b. Colours（色，いろ）: colour the ○ below yourself.

［A］白い	しろ(い)	［N］白	しろ	○ white
黒い	くろ(い)	黒	くろ	○ black
赤い	あか(い)	赤	あか	○ red
青い	あお(い)	青	あお	○ blue
黄色い	きいろ(い)	黄色＝黄	き(いろ)	○ yellow
茶色い	ちゃいろ(い)	茶色＝茶	ちゃ(いろ)	○ brown
		緑	みどり	○ green
		紫	むらさき	○ purple
		ピンク		○ pink
		オレンジ		○ orange
		黄緑色	きみどりいろ	○ yellowish green
		灰色	はいいろ	○ gray
		金色	きんいろ	○ gold
		銀色	ぎんいろ	○ silver

こい		dark	↔	うすい		light
明るい	あかるい	bright	↔	暗い	くらい	dark

〜と同じような │色│です。　　*(It has) the same kind of colour/*
　　おな　　　　　│形│　　　　　　*shape as 〜*
　　　　　　　　いろ
　　　　　　　　かたち

① 職員：どんな色のかばんですか。
　しょくいん

　　客：あ、この本と同じような色なんです。
　きゃく　　　　ほん

② ☎A：どんな箱。↗

　　B：ええと、リーさんのと同じような形で、赤いんだ。👕
　　　　　　　　　　　　　　　　　　あか

c. Size（サイズ）:

長さ	＝	〜メートル	〜 m
なが		〜センチ	〜 cm
		〜ミリ	〜 mm

CN

169

大きさ＝
縦	たて	*depth, length*
横	よこ	*width*
高さ	たか（さ）	*height*
厚さ	あつ（さ）	*thickness*
幅	はば	*width*

cf. 厚い ↔ うすい

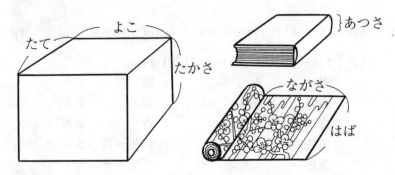

～ぐらいの	大きさです。	*(It's) about the size of ～*
	長さ	*length*
	高さ	*height*
	厚さ	*thickness*

～さ ⇨L10GNⅥ

① その時計はたまごぐらいの大きさです。

② その辞書は人の手ぐらいの大きさです。

170

＜*Strategies*＞

S-1. How to enquire about something you left behind

a. To enquire about a lost article by telephone, first call the office and tell them that you left something behind:

① 客：もしもし、常総バスの営業所ですか。
きゃく　　　　　じょうそう　　　えいぎょうしょ
　　Hello, is that the Joso bus office?

職員：はい。
しょくいん
　　Yes, it is.

客：あの、けさバスの中に忘れ物をしたんですが。
　　　　　　　　なか　わす　もの
　　I lost something in the bus this morning.

職員：はい。係のものとかわりますので、お待ちください。
　　　　かかり　　　　　　　　　　　　ま
　　I see. I'll put you through to the person in charge, so please hold on.

② 客：あの、上野駅ですか。
　　　　うえのえき
　　Er..., is that Ueno station?

職員1：はい。
　　Yes, it is.

客：あのう、遺失物係をお願いします。
　　　　いしつぶつがかり　　　ねが
　　The lost-property office please.

職員1：少々お待ちください。
　　　　しょうしょう
　　Just a moment please.

　　　　・　　・　　・

職員2：もしもし。遺失物係ですが。
　　Hello, this is the lost-property office.

客：あの、きのう常磐線の電車の中にかばんを忘れちゃったんですが。
　　　　　　　じょうばんせん　でんしゃ
　　Well, I lost my bag in a train on the Joban line yesterday.

職員2：はい。
　　I see.

After that, you'll need to explain what you lost when and where.

CN

b. To ask for further help, the polite request forms below are useful:

$$\sim \text{[V-te]} \quad \left| \begin{array}{l} \text{くださいますか。／くださいませんか。} \\ \text{いただけますか。／いただけませんか。} \end{array} \right.$$

Could you please ～ ? /*Would you mind ～ ing?*

Negative requests are more indirect and therefore more polite than affirmative ones. Compare the range of variation below: ⇨GN I，II

$$\sim て \quad \left| \begin{array}{l} \text{くれますか。} \\ \text{くれませんか。} \\ \text{くださいますか。} \\ \text{くださいませんか。} \\ \text{くださいますでしょうか。} \\ \text{くださいませんでしょうか。} \end{array} \right. \qquad \sim て \quad \left| \begin{array}{l} \text{もらえますか。} \\ \text{もらえませんか。} \\ \text{いただけますか。} \\ \text{いただけませんか。} \\ \text{いただけますでしょうか。} \\ \text{いただけませんでしょうか。} \end{array} \right.$$

Could you please ～ ?   *Would you mind ～ ?*

① 電話番号、教えて │ くれますか。📄➡️⬇️
　　でんわばんごう　おし │ くれる。↗ 😊➡️⬇️

Could you give me the telephone number?

② ペンを貸してくださいませんか。📄⬆️
　　　　か
Would you mind lending me a pen?

③ まどを開けて │ もらえますか。📄➡️⬇️
　　　　あ │ もらえる。↗ 😊➡️⬇️

Can you open the window?

④ もう一度説明していただけませんでしょうか。📄⬆️
　　いちどせつめい
Would you mind explaining it again please?

S-2. How to answer questions

When enquiring about a lost article, you may be asked when and where (which bus, which train etc.) you lost it and what it looks like (⇨CN2, S-4), as in the questions and answers below:

客：きのうバスにかばんを　　　　*I lost a bag in the bus yesterday.*
きゃく
　　忘れちゃったんですが。
　　わす

職員：どこ行き｜。↗
しょくいん　い｜のバス。↗
　　　　｜のバスですか。↗

What destination?

客：大学正門行きです。
きゃく　だいがくせいもん

University Main Entrance.

職員：何時ごろ｜。↗
なんじ　｜ですか。↗

Around what time?

客：ええと、大学正門着が
　　4時半のバスです。
ちゃく
じはん

Let me see, It's the bus that arrives at the Main Entrance of the University around 4:30.

職員：あ、そう｜。↘
　　　　｜ですか。↘
　　　で、どんなかばん｜。↗
　　　　　　　　　　　｜ですか。↗

I see.

What kind of bag?

S-3. How to confirm information —3.

As we saw in L4 and L12, there are several ways of confirming information.

a. Repeating a word or a expression ⇨L4 S-4a

A：このへんに電話ありますか。
　　　　　　　でんわ
B：あ、食堂の自動販売機のとなりにありますよ。
　　　しょくどう　じどうはんばいき
A：自動販売機のとなり。↗／↘
　　じどうはんばいき
B：ええ。

b. Adding **か** or **ね** to a word or an expression ⇨L4 S-4b

A：どのくらいかかりますか。

B：そうですね。20分はかかると思いますけど。
　　　　　　　　　ぷん　　　　　　おも

A：20分です｜か。↗／↘
　　　　　　　｜ね。↗

B：ええ。

With rising intonation, **か** shows uncertainty. **ね**（rising intonation only）is used to seek agreement.

c. Saying **はい** or **ええ** to show that you've taken in the information:

> A：すみません。電話番号、教えていただけますか。
> でんわばんごう　おし
>
> B：はい。７４の……
>
> A：<u>はい。</u>
>
> B：５９４６です。
>
> A：<u>はい。</u>どうも。

d. To indicate that you didn't get it, use **はあ↗** , **え↗** 🅒 or 「**あの、すみません。もう一度お願いします。** 📖 (*Can you say that again, please.*)」
いちど　おねが

> A：井上医院の電話番号、わかりますか。
> いのうえいいん
>
> B：ええと、５２の３１８１ですよ。
>
> A：<u>あの、すみません。もう一度お願いします。</u>
>
> B：ごお・にいの、さん・いち・はち・いち。
>
> A：わかりました。どうも。

e. Rephrasing

> ① A：ええと、８時４０分ごろ、大学正門に着いたんですが。
> じ　ふん　だいがくせいもん　つ
> *It arrived at the main entrance of the university around 8:40.*
>
> B：<u>じゃ、松見駅、８時７分のバスですね。</u>
> まつみえき　ふん
> *So it's the 8:07 bus from MATSUMI station.*
>
> A：あ、はい。そうだと思います。
> おも
> *Ah, yes. That's right.*
>
> ② A：茶色の紙袋です。中に本が入ってるんですけど。
> ちゃいろ　かみふくろ　なか　ほん　はい
> *It's a brown paper bag. There's a book inside.*
>
> B：<u>本が入った、茶の紙袋ね。</u>
> ちゃ
> *A brown paper bag with a book in it.*
>
> A：ええ。
> *Yes.*

S-4. How to describe something

a. 形（かたち, *Shape*）: ⇨CN2a

① **A：どんな形のかばんですか。**   *What sort of bag?*

    B：丸くて大きいかばんです。   *It's a large, round bag.*

② **A：どんな箱ですか。**   *What type of box?*

    B：小さい三角の箱です。   *A small triangular box.*

③ **A：どんなふうとうですか。**   *What type of envelope?*

    B：このぐらいの大きさの白いふうとうです。   *A white envelope of about this size.*

b. 色（いろ, *Colour*）: ⇨CN2b

① **A：何色のかばんですか。**   *What colour's the bag?*

    B：赤と青のしまのかばんです。   *It's a bag with red and blue stripes.*

② **A：どんな袋ですか。**   *What type of bag?*

    B：白い紙袋です。   *A white paper bag.*

③ **A：どんなさいふですか。**   *What type of wallet?*

    B：茶色の皮のさいふです。   *A brown leather wallet.*

c. 大きさ（おおきさ, *Size*）: ⇨CN2c

① **A：どのぐらいの大きさですか。**

    What size?

    B：たて５０センチ、よこ３０センチぐらいです。

    About 50cm long and 30cm wide.

② **A：どんな箱ですか。**

    What type of box?

    B：黄色い箱で、辞書ぐらいの大きさです。

    A yellow box about the size of a dictionary.

CN

③　A：どんな袋ですか。
　　　　What type of bag?

　　B：たてよこ４０センチぐらいの黒い袋です。
　　　　A black bag of around 40cm by 40cm.

d. 何が入っているか（*Content*）:

①　A：中に何が入っていますか。
　　　　What's in it?

　　B：ええと、銀色の時計が入っています。
　　　　Uh... a silver-coloured watch.

②　A：どんな袋ですか。
　　　　What type of bag?

　　B：むらさきの紙袋で、中に辞書が入っています。
　　　　A purple paper bag with a dictionary inside.

S-5.　How to express one's feelings

　　When someone wants to show his/her feelings, s/he may do it, in the folowing way:

a. Relief

　　　A：茶色の紙袋です。
　　　B：届いてますよ。
　　　A：ああ（**dangling**の印）、よかった。

b. Puzzlement

　　　A：茶色の紙袋です。
　　　B：ありませんけど。
　　　A：ええっ、こまったな／わ（**女**）。

c. Joy

　　やった！（I did it.）is used for instance when you have passed the enter examination.

第15課

本を借りる
ほん　か
Borrowing a book

OBJECTIVES:

GRAMMAR

Ⅰ. 〜てみる: *to try doing*

Ⅱ. 〜ておく: *doing something for a future purpose*

Ⅲ. 〜てある: *a state resulting from the action of the verb*

Ⅳ. 〜ていく: *doing something and then going*

　〜てくる: *doing something and then coming*

Ⅴ. Imperatives

Ⅵ. 何か，だれか，どこか: <question word>＋か

　何も，だれも，どこも: <question word>＋も

Ⅶ. いつも，よく，ときどき，

　たまに，あまり，めったに : *adverbs of frequency*

Ⅷ. 〜中（じゅう／ちゅう）: *throughout 〜, in the middle of 〜*

CONVERSATION

<General Information>

1. University libraries

<Strategies>

S-1. How to start a conversation —6. After not having seen each other for a long time

S-2. How to talk about other people

S-3. How to ask for advice on books

S-4. How to thank for/decline offers of help

S-5. How to ask how long you can borrow something

Model Conversation

Characters ：Tanaka(田中), Suzuki(鈴木)

Situation ：Tanaka-san asks Suzuki-san's advice about books in the library and then borrows a book.

Flow-chart ：

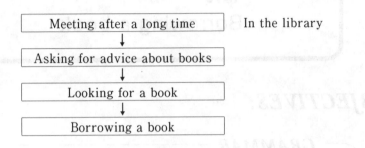

Meeting after a long time	In the library
↓
Asking for advice about books
↓
Looking for a book
↓
Borrowing a book

― 資料室で ―

田　中：失礼します。

鈴　木：やあ、田中さん。ひさしぶり。

田　中：どうもごぶさたしてます。

鈴　木：どう。論文、進んでる。

田　中：ええ、どうにか。

鈴　木：きょうは、リサさんは。

田　中：あ、東京なんです。どこかの会社にインタビューに行くって言ってましたけど。

鈴　木：ふうん。

　　　　　　＊　　　　　＊　　　　　＊

田　中：きょうは、ちょっと本のことで……。

鈴　木：どんなこと。

田　中：ええと、エキスパート・システムについてさがしてるんですけど、何かありますか。

鈴　木：そうね。これなんか、どうかな。(Showing a book)

田　中：これ、私に読めるでしょうか。

鈴　木：うん、基本的な概念の説明だから、だいじょうぶだと思うけど。

田　中：じゃ、読んでみます。

　　　　　　＊　　　　　＊　　　　　＊

178

鈴　木：そうそう。あと、医学の診断システムの本もたしか……。
　　　　（Looking for the book）
田　中：すみません、お手数かけて。
鈴　木：おかしいな。いつもはここに置いてあるんだけど。
田　中：そうですか。
鈴　木：だれか借りてってるんじゃないかな。ちょっと待ってて。
田　中：はい。
鈴　木：ええとね。（Checking the records）
田　中：はい。
鈴　木：あ、やっぱり貸出し中だ。5日まで、だめだね。
田　中：そうですか。じゃ、そのころ、もう一度来てみますから。
鈴　木：そうね。

　　　　　＊　　　　＊　　　　＊

田　中：じゃ、きょうは、この本だけにします。
鈴　木：うん。じゃ、このノートに書いといて。
田　中：はい。ええと、2週間でしたね。
鈴　木：そう。忘れるなよ。
田　中：はい。じゃ、失礼します。
鈴　木：うん。じゃ、また。

Report

<田中さんの日記>

　エキスパートシステムについて何も知らないので、何か基本的な本を読みたいと思った。そこで、情報工学の資料室に行ってみた。

　そこには専門の本や雑誌が置いてあって、ほかの研究科の学生も利用できる。貸出し中の場合は予約もできる。ときどき、鈴木さんが貸出しの仕事を手伝っている。

　ちょうど鈴木さんがいたので相談してみたら、いろいろさがしてくれた。鈴木さんがすすめてくれた本はちょっとむずかしいと思ったが、ほかのは貸出し中だったので、その一冊だけ借りてきた。2週間以内に全部読めるかな……。

New Words and Expressions

Words in the conversation

資料室	しりょうしつ	*library*
論文	ろんぶん	*thesis, dissertation*
進む	すすむ	*to advance*
どうにか		*somehow*
どこか		*somewhere*
インタビュー		*interview*
エキスパート・システム		*expert system*（a type of computer software system）
～について		*about, on*
何か	なにか	*something*
基本的（な）	きほんてき（な）	*basic*
概念	がいねん	*concept*
説明	せつめい	*explanation*
あと		*also*
医学	いがく	*medical science*
診断システム	しんだんシステム	*diagnostic system*
手数	てすう	*trouble, bother*
おかしい		*strange*
いつも		*usually, always*
置く	おく	*to put down, to place*
だれか		*somebody*
借りる	かりる	*to borrow*
やっぱり		*as expected, after all*
貸出し中 /貸し出し中	かしだしちゅう	*on loan*
そのころ		*about that time*
ノート		*notebook*

<Expressions in the conversation>

ひさしぶり。	*I haven't seen you for a long time.* ☻
	⇨CN S-1

ごぶさたしています。   *I have not seen you for a long time.* 🔲
⇨CN S-1

どう。↗論文、進んでる。↗   *How are you getting on with your thesis?* 🅔
⇨CN S-1

〜って言ってましたけど。   *(S/he) said (that)* 〜 ⇨CN S-2
　　〜と言う ⇨L9GN Ⅱ
In informal speech, 〜と言う is often contracted to 〜って言う.

ふうん。↗   *Really.* 🅔

ちょっと本のことで……。   *(I'd like to ask) about a book.*
　　ちょっと [N] のことで indicates a topic. ⇨L13CN S-2

これなんか、どうかな。↗   *How about something like this?* 🅔
　　[N] なんか implies that the choice is not restricted to [N].

読んでみます。   *I'll try to read it.*
　　[V-te] みる ⇨GN Ⅰ

あと、医学の診断システムの本もたし   *Also, there's a book about diagnostic*
か……。   *systems, too, I seem to remember.*
　　あと [N] もたしか shows that you recall another [N].

すみません、お手数かけて。   *Sorry to trouble you.* ⇨CN S-4

いつもはここに置いてあるんだけど。   *Normally it's placed here, but (I can't find it).* 🅔
　　[V-te] ある ⇨GN Ⅲ

だれか借りてってるんじゃないかな。   *Someone must have borrowed it.* 🅔
　　[V-te] いく ⇨GN Ⅳ
In informal speech, 〜ていっている（[V-te] いく ＋ ている）is often contracted to 〜てってる.

ちょっと待ってて。   *Just a moment.* 🅔
In informal speech, 〜ていて is often shortened to 〜てて.

もう一度来てみますから。   *I'll come back later.*

この本だけにします。   *I'll take only this book.*
　　[N] にする shows one's decision. ⇨L3GN Ⅲ

このノートに書いといて。   *Write it in this notebook.* 🅔

MC

181

[V-te] おく ⇨GN Ⅱ

In conversation, ～ておいて is often shortened to ～といて.

2 週間でしたね。↗   *It's for 2 weeks, isn't it?*
  しゅうかん
  　～でしたね asks for confirmation. ⇨CN S-5

忘れるなよ。↗   *Don't forget, OK?* 🔵👕
  わす
  　[V-(r)u] な ⇨GN Ⅴ

Men often use ～なよ↗ for giving a friendly warning.

Words in the report

何も （～ない）	なにも	*nothing*
情報工学	じょうほうこうがく	*information technology*
雑誌	ざっし	*magazine*
研究科	けんきゅうか	*graduate course*
利用する	りようする	*to make use of*
～の場合	～のばあい	*in case of ～*
予約	よやく	*booking, reservation*
ときどき		*sometimes*
仕事	しごと	*work, job*
手伝う	てつだう	*to help*
ちょうど		*by chance, happen to*
相談する	そうだんする	*to consult, to discuss*
すすめる		*to recommend*
～以内に	～いないに	*(with) in* (time)
全部	ぜんぶ	*all*

＜Expressions in the report＞

貸出し中の場合は   *If the book is already on loan,*
かしだ ちゅう ばあい

その一冊だけ借りてきた。   *(I) took out only one book.*
いっさつ　　　か
  　[V-te] くる ⇨GN Ⅳ

Grammar Notes

I. 〜てみる: *to try doing*

Examples

① ちょっと食べてみてください。
Please try it/have a taste.

② このコートを着てみてもいいですか。
Can I try this coat on?

【Explanation】

[V-te] みる means 'to do something and see how it goes/what will happen'. The difference between 食べる and 食べてみる is illustrated in the pictures below: The man wants the woman's opinion on the taste of the food he's prepared, so he asks her to taste it: 食べてみてください. In this situation, 食べてください would be inappropriate; however, he would use 食べてください *Please eat* to ask his guests at table to start dinner, although he could also say 食べてみてください *Please try the food and see (if you like it)*.

In ②, the customer is asking the shop assistant if she can try the coat on:

[V-te]みる can be used with various endings such as 食べてみてください, 食べてみたいです, 食べてみてもいいですか, 食べてみた, 食べてみたら.

Ⅱ．〜ておく: doing something for a future purpose

Examples

① **ガールフレンドが来るので、部屋をそうじしておきます。**
Since my girlfriend is coming, I'm cleaning my room (so she won't think that I am a slob).

② **ジュースを冷蔵庫に入れておきました。**
I put some juice in the refrigerator (so that we can have a cold one later).

③ （after eating at a restaurant）
A：あれっ、さいふを忘れた。　　　*Oh, I forgot to bring my wallet.*

B：じゃ、私が払っておきます。　　*In that case, I'll pay (for the moment).*

④ **A：窓を閉めましょうか。**　　　　*Shall I close the window?*

B：いや、そのまま* 開けておいてください。　　　　*そのまま　*as it is*
No, please leave it open (as it is).

【*Explanation*】

When **おく** is attached to the -te form of another verb, it expresses the following:

1) doing something for the future (①②), or on a temporary basis (③)

そうじしておきます in ① implies a purpose for the action of cleaning; for instance, the speaker may want his girlfriend to feel comfortable or prevent her from realizing how messy he really is. Because ～ておく usually implies that the action of the verb relates to a future event, 私が払っておきます (③) usually indicates that B expects A to repay him later, whereas 私が払います has no such implication.

ガールフレンドが来るので
そうじしておきます。

2) to leave a state for a future purpose (④)

In ④, a woman notices an open window and offers to close it; the man tells her to leave it open:

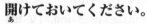

開けておいてください。

閉めましょうか。

開けておいて
ください。

185

[V-te] おく is used with various endings such as 開けておいてください, 開けておきたいです, 開けておいてもいいですか, 開けておいた, 開けておいたら, 開けておかない.

In casual speech, 〜ておく is often shortened to 〜とく: 書いとく for 書いておく, 開けとく for 開けておく etc.

Ⅲ. 〜てある: a state resulting from the action of the verb

Examples

① ドアが開けてあります。
The door has been opened.

② ジュースが冷蔵庫に入れてあります。
Juice has been put in the fridge.

③ ここに住所が書いてあります。
The address is written here.

【*Explanation*】

1. The meaning of 〜てある

[V-te] ある expresses a state resulting from an action; in ②, the state resulting from some unspecified person having put juice into the refrigerator.

2. The difference between 〜ている and 〜てある

You have come across a similar expression, [V-te] いる. ⇨L8GNV; what's the difference?

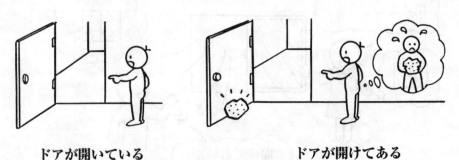

ドアが開いている　　　　　　ドアが開けてある

Both ドアが開いている and ドアが開けてある indicate that the door is open, but あけてある implies that someone is responsible for that state.

＜thing＞が《＋を verb》てある implies that someone has brought about the state. ＜thing＞が《－を verb》ている ignores any actor or force that may have brought about the state.

The table below shows the relation between expressions of change/action and of a state. Note that 開く is a《－を verb》 whereas 開ける is a《＋を verb》. ⇨L11GNⅢ

something が《－を verb》ている　vs　something が《＋を verb》てある		
	～ている	～てある
Change / Action	something が《－を verb》 ドア　　が　　開いた *The door opened*	someone が something を《＋を verb》 （someone が）ドア　　を　　開けた *(Someone) opened the door*
State (result of change or action)	something が[V-te]いる ドア　が　開いている *The door is open*	something が [V-te] ある ドア　　が　　開けてある *The door has been opened*

From the table, you can infer that ジュースが入れてある in ② implies that someone put it in.

ジュースを入れる。　　　→　　　ジュースが入れてある。

(Someone) puts juice in (the refregerator).　　*Juice is in (the fridge).*

3. The relationship between ～ておく and ～てある

You may now wish to rethink the relation between [V-te] おく and [V-te] ある as follows.

ジュースを入れておく。---- the result remains ---- ジュースが入れてある。

(Someone) puts juice in (the fridge).　　　　　　　*Juice is in (the fridge).*

187

Note that the verbs used before **ある** are not only 《＋ を verbs》 but also controllable. For example, if you find money dropped on the road, you will say:

○ あっ、お金が落ちている。　　　（落ちる《−をVerb》）

× あっ、お金が落としてある。　　（落とす《＋をVerb》）

This is because the action **お金を落とす** *to drop some money* is normally done unintentionally.（If it were done intentionally for some reason, however, the second sentence could be used.）

Note that [**V-te**] **ある** is used with various endings, ex. **開けてあった**, **開けてあったら**, **開けてない**.

The verbs used with **ある** are 《＋ を verbs》 whose actions can be controlled by the actor.

Ⅳ. ～ていく: *doing something and then going*
　　 ～てくる: *doing something and then coming*

Examples

① リサさんに花を持っていきます。
I will take some flowers for Lisa-san. (lit. I will pick up flowers and go to Lisa-san.)

② A：この本を借りていってもいいですか。
May I take this book out?

B：すみません。ここで読んでください。
Sorry, please read it here.

③ 電話をかけてきました。
I phoned and then came here.

④ この手紙を出してきてください。
Please go and mail this letter.

【*Explanation*】

いく means *to go* and **くる** means *to come*.

[**V-te**] **いく** means *to do something and go away*; **持っていく** in ① means *to pick up and go* and **借りていく** in ② *to borrow and go*.

[V-te] **くる** means *to do something and come/come back*. The starting point of coming is not always clear (③), but in ④, **出してくる** means *going to the postbox and coming back*.

By adding **いく** or **くる** to [V-te], you can indicate the direction of the action, as shown by the arrows in the following pictures:

借りていく
[V-te] **いく**
to borrow and go

借りてくる
[V-te] **くる**
to borrow and come

借りてくる
[V-te] **くる**
*to go and borrow
(and come back)*

Like [V-te] **みる** and [V-te] **おく**, [V-te] **いく／くる** are used with various endings 持っていってください, 持っていきたいです, 持っていった, 持っていったら, 持っていかない。

Note that in the spoken language **～ていく** is often shortened to **～てく** e.g. in 借りてく for 借りていく.

V. Imperatives

Examples

① **止まれ。**　　　　　　　　　*Stop!*

② **進め。**　　　　　　　　　*Move on!*

③ **ごみをすてるな。**　　　　*Don't litter!*

④ **飲んだら、運転するな。**　　*When you drink, don't drive!*

⑤ **お医者さんはたばこをすうなと
言いました。**　　　　　　　*The doctor told me not to smoke!*

⑥ **勉強しなさい。**　　　　　*Study!*

GN

【*Explanation*】

Imperatives (commands) are blunt expressions often implying a high -handed attitude. For the sake of brevity, however, they are used in signs, slogans etc. as in ①～④ above.

Highers often use this form to Lowers (fathers to their children, etc.), especially with the particle **よ** attached to soften the bluntness, ex. **行けよ**, **来るなよ**。 Imperatives are often used by men in casual speech, whereas women rarely use them.

⑤ (A formal style sentence) illustrates the use of the imperative form in sentences reporting speech.

Another type of imperative is **[V (base)] なさい** (⑥), which is used only for positive commands like **勉強しなさい** (instead of **勉強しろ**), **行きなさい** (instead of **行け**), and **止まりなさい** (instead of **止まれ**). **なさい** expressions are often used in instructions on exam papers and by mothers telling their children what to do.

Imperative form			
[V-(r)u] (Dictionary form)		Imperative form	
		Positive	Negative
		-u → -e	dic. form ＋ na
Group Ⅰ	tomaru *to stop* 止まる susumu *to move on* 進む tatsu *to stand* 立つ	tomare 止まれ susume 進め tate 立て	tomaru na 止まるな susumu na 進むな tatsu na 立つな
		-ru → -ro	dic. form ＋ na
Group Ⅱ	suteru *to throw away* 捨てる miseru *to show* 見せる taberu *to eat* 食べる	sutero 捨てろ misero 見せろ tabero 食べろ	suteru na 捨てるな miseru na 見せるな taberu na 食べるな

			irregular	dic. form ＋ na
Group Ⅲ	suru する	*to do*	shiro しろ	suru na するな
	unten suru 運転する	*to drive*	unten shiro 運転しろ	unten suru na 運転するな
	kuru 来る	*to come*	koi 来い	kuru na 来るな
	motte kuru 持ってくる	*to bring*	motte koi 持ってこい	motte kuru na 持ってくるな

Ⅵ. 何か，だれか，どこか: ＜question word＞＋か
何も，だれも，どこも: ＜question word＞＋も (in negative sentence)
なに

Examples

① 田中さんはノートに何か（を）書きました。
たなか　　　　　　　　　　　　　　　　　　　か
Tanaka-san wrote something in the notebook.

② だれか（が）ドアをノックしています。　　*Someone is knocking on the door.*

③ どこかで休みましょう。　　*Let's take a rest somewhere.*
　　　　　やす

④ 何も食べたくありません。　　*I don't want to eat anything.*
なに　た

⑤ だれも来ませんでした。　　*Nobody came.*
　　　き

⑥ あしたはどこ（へ）も行きません。　　*I'm not going anywhere tomorrow.*
　　　　　　　　　　い

⑦ A：最近、何か映画を見ましたか。　　*Have you seen any movies lately?*
　　さいきん　えいが　み

　B：いいえ、何も見ていません。　　*No, I haven't seen any.*

⑧ A：夏休みはどこか海へ行きましたか。
　　なつやす　　　うみ
Did you go to any beach resort during the summer vacation?

　B：いいえ、どこへも行きませんでした。　　*No, I didn't go anywhere.*

GN

【*Explanation*】

1. ＜question word＞＋か: 何か，だれか，どこか (①②③)

The combination ＜question word＞＋か means *some...* in positive sentences and *any...* in question sentences; it is not used in negative statements.

何	*what?*		何か	*something, anything*
だれ	*who?*		だれか	*somebody, anybody*
どこ	*where?*	＋ か →	どこか	*somewhere, anywhere*
いつ	*when?*		いつか	*someday, anyday*
どれ	*which?*		どれか	*one of them*
どちら	*which?, where?*		どちらか	*one of the two, somewhere/anywhere*

2. ＜question word＞＋も: 何も　だれも　どこも (④⑤⑥)

On the other hand ＜question word＞＋も is used usually in negative sentences.

何	*what?*		何も〜ない	*nothing*
だれ	*who?*		だれも〜ない	*nobody*
どこ	*where?*	＋ も →	どこも〜ない	*nowhere*
どれ	*which*		どれも〜ない	*nothing*
どちら	*which*		どちらも〜ない	*neither of the two*

3. Use of particles

In spoken Japanese, the structure particles **が** and **を** are usually deleted after ＜question word＞＋か or ＜question word＞＋も; You can also leave out **に** or **へ** if the meaning is clear without these particles. However, other structure particles, (で, から, まで, and と) are always required. ⇨L3GNⅦ

4. ＜question word＞＋か modifying nouns

As you can see from ⑦ and ⑧, these expressions can also be used to modify nouns, in which use they correspond to English *some, any*.

▼ Note that structure particles are never used before nouns in this use:

　○　何か映画を見ましたか。
　　　えいが　み

　×　何か<u>を</u>映画を見ましたか。

Ⅶ. いつも，よく，ときどき，たまに: adverbs of frequency
あまり，めったに

If someone asks you "How often do you play tennis after class?", you can choose your answer from the following:

You play everyday	いつも	する	*always*
every other day	よく	する	*often*
once a week	ときどき	する	*sometimes*
once a month	たまに	する	*once in a while*
once a month	あまり	しない	*not very often*
a few times a year	めったに	しない	*rarely*
not at all	ぜんぜん	しない	*never*

The above are just some examples of how to express frequency, as they are based on the speaker's subjective assessment. Depending on the speaker's perception, the same frequency, e.g. once a week, can be presented as *often* or *sometimes*.

いつも，毎日， よく	ときどき	たまに， あまり～ない	めったに～ない，ぜんぜん～ない ほとんど～ない

Ⅷ. ～中（じゅう／ちゅう）: *throughout～, in the middle of ～*

Examples

① きのうは一日中雨が降っていました。
　いちにちじゅうあめ　ふ
It was raining all day yesterday.

② この大学には世界中から留学生が来ます。
　だいがく　せかいじゅう　りゅうがくせい　き
Foreign students from all over the world come to this university.

③ この道路は工事中です。
　どうろ　こうじちゅう
This road is under construction.

GN

193

---

④ その本は貸出中です。
ほん　かしだしちゅう
The book is on loan.

【*Explanation*】

～中 has the following three uses〔be careful to note that the pronunciation of 中 differs depending on its usage〕:

1. ＜period of time＞中 (pronounced: じゅう)

＜period of time＞中 indicates that an event takes place, or a situation holds during/throughout a certain period of time（①）.

一日中（いちにちじゅう）	*the whole day, throughout the day*
一年中（いちねんじゅう）	*the whole year, throughout the year*
今週中（こんしゅうじゅう／ちゅう）	*during/throughout this week*
午前中（ごぜんちゅう）	*a.m. is exceptional in that 中 is prono* ～ちゅう.

2. ＜place＞中 (pronounced: じゅう)

＜place＞中 indicates the whole of ＜place＞（②）.

世界中（せかいじゅう）	*all over/throughout the world*
日本中（にほんじゅう）	*all over/throughout Japan*
部屋中（へやじゅう）	*the whole room*

3. ＜activity＞中 (pronounced: ちゅう)（③④）

＜activity＞中 indicates that an activity is in the middle of being conducted:

工事中（こうじちゅう）	*under construction*
会議中（かいぎちゅう）	*meeting in session*
貸出中（かしだしちゅう）	*on loan*
使用中（しようちゅう）	*in use*

Conversation Notes

General Information

1. University libraries

Japanese universities usually have a central library (**中央図書館, ちゅうおうとしょかん**) and several departmental libraries. Some departments also have a number of smaller libraries for special subjects called **資料室（しりょうしつ）** or **図書室（としょしつ）**.

Libraries are usually closed on Sundays, national holidays and over the New Year. Opening hours differ from library to library.

Students are normally required to show their ID card at the entrance.

a. Looking for books

Like public libraries, university libraries usually have open stacks, a system called **開架式（かいかしき）**; closed stacks are referred to as **閉架式（へいかしき）**. Whereas you have access to open stacks yourself, you have to ask a librarian (**図書館員, としょかんいん／司書, ししょ**) to get books for you from closed stacks.

In Japanese libraries, books are classified according to the 10 subject areas listed below (with subclassification within each subject), and books are numbered and placed according to this system. ⇨L11CN1

0 0 0	総記	そうき	*general description*
1 0 0	哲学	てつがく	*philosophy*
2 0 0	歴史	れきし	*history*
3 0 0	社会科学	しゃかいかがく	*social sciences*
4 0 0	自然科学	しぜんかがく	*natural sciences*
5 0 0	技術・工学	ぎじゅつ・こうがく	*technology/engineering*
6 0 0	産業	さんぎょう	*industry*
7 0 0	芸術	げいじゅつ	*art*
8 0 0	言語	げんご	*language*
9 0 0	文学	ぶんがく	*literature*

You can locate a book by using the card catalogue or the on-line computer search system. Librarians can also provide information.

b. Borrowing books

To borrow from the library, take the books to the issue desk with your ID card. In the smaller libraries of the university, you normally have to fill in a borrowing slip with your personal data. At a public library, you may need to apply for a borrowing card.

Usually, you can borrow several books at once for a period of two or three weeks, with extensions possible thereafter. Failure to return or extend books by the deadline may result in loss of borrowing privileges.

Items not available for borrowing can be photocopied in the library at your expense.

If a book is on loan, you can usually reserve it. Books that are not stocked in the library of your university may be available through interlibrary loan for which you will be charged (postage is payable).

[Flow-chart for borrowing books]

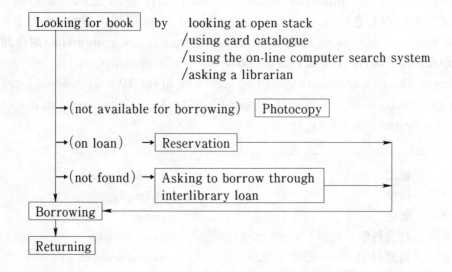

＜*Strategies*＞

S-1.　How to start a conversation —6.: After a long time

a. When you meet someone you haven't seen for some time, you can start the conversation with the following expressions:

ひさしぶり	（ね。）🗨👤 （だね。）🗨👤 です（ね。）📄

I haven't seen you for a long time.

おひさしぶりです。📄⬆

しばらく	（ね。）🗨👤 （だね。）🗨👤 です（ね。）📄

If s/he is your senior, use the following:

ごぶさた	しています。📄⬆（polite） しております。📄⬆（more polite） いたしております。📄⬆（most polite）

You can ask how s/he is:

元気。↗ 🗨　　　　　　　　　　　*How are you?*
元気ですか。↗ 📄
お元気ですか。↗ 📄⬆

If asked how you are, you can reply with **おかげさまで** *thanks to you*, in formal situations, and then ask the same question. For informal situations, **なんとか** *somehow* can be used.

① 📄 山下：先生、ごぶさたしてます。

　　山下（やました）　木村（きむら）　先生（せんせい）

　　木村：やあ、山下くん、しばらく。

　　山下：お元気ですか。

　　木村：うん、ありがとう。山下くんは。↗

　　山下：ええ、おかげさまで。

②ⓒ山下：やあ。田中さん、しばらく。

田中：あら、山下さん、ひさしぶり。

山下：元気。↗

田中：ええ。山下さんは。↗

山下：うん、なんとか。

b. In social conversation, it is usual to enquire about how someone is getting on. You can start the conversation as follows:

どう。↗ ⓒ	*How are things?*
どうですか。↗ 🖥	
いかがですか。↗ 🖥⬆	

You can mention the topic, adding a suitable enquiry:

〜、	進んでますか。🖥	*(How) are you getting on with 〜 ?*
	うまくいってますか。🖥	*How is 〜 going?*
	終わりましたか。🖥	*Have you finished 〜 ?*
	よくなりましたか。🖥	*Are you well now?* (after illness)
	慣れましたか。🖥	*Have you got used to 〜 ?*

The above expressions can also be used in the casual style as follows:

〜、	進んでる。↗ ⓒ	
	うまくいってる。↗ ⓒ	
	終わった。↗ ⓒ	
	よくなった。↗ ⓒ	
	慣れた。↗ ⓒ	

When asked these questions, you can reply with the following:

おかげさまで 🖥⬆	*very well; thanks to you*	
まあまあ ⓒ	*not too bad*	↑
なんとか／どうにか 🖥／ⓒ	*somehow or other*	(positive)
なかなか 🖥／ⓒ	*not so well*	(negative)
ぜんぜん 🖥／ⓒ	*not at all*	↓

① 鈴木：どう。↗　論文、進んでる。↗

田中：ええ、どうにか。

② 田中：いかがですか。↗　かぜ、よくなりました。↗

鈴木：いや、ぜんぜん。

You can also ask with just 〜のほうは:

③ 鈴木：どう。↗　論文のほうは。↗

田中：ええ、おかげさまで。

④ 田中：いかがですか。↗　かぜのほうは。↗

鈴木：いや、なかなか。

S-2. How to talk about other people

You can enquire how others are doing:

〜さん	は。↗ 🇨
	（は）どうしてる。↗ 🇨
	（は）どうしてますか。↗ 🇪

How is (someone)?

When asked about others, you can report what they've told you as follows:
⇨ L9GN Ⅱ

〜って	（言ってた。）🇨
	言っていました。🇪

S/he said (that) 〜

① 鈴木：きょうは、リサさんは。↗

What's Lisa-san up to today?

田中：あ、東京なんです。どこかの会社にインタビューに行くって言ってましたけど。

She's gone to Tokyo. She said she was going to have an interview with some firm (there).

②　山下：田中さん、どうしてる。↗
　　やました　たなか
　　　How is Tanaka-san?

　　リサ：今、論文ですごくいそがしいって言ってたけど。
　　　　　いま　ろんぶん　　　　　　　　　　　　　　　　　い
　　　She said she's terribly busy with her thesis.

S-3. How to ask for advice on books

a. If you are trying to find some books that are useful for your work, you can ask for advice as follows:

～について	何かありませんか。	🔲 *Is there anything on ～ ?*
	なに	
	さがしているんですけど。	🔲 *I'm looking for something on ～.*

You can ask if a recommended book is not too difficult for you:

これ、私に読める	かな。↘ 🔘	*I wonder if I can read this.*
わたし　よ	かしら。↘ 🔘🚹	
	でしょうか。↘ 🔲	

田中：ええと、エキスパート・システムについて探してるんですけど。
　　　　　　　　　　　　　　　　　　　　　　　さが
　　Um, I am looking for something on expert systems.

鈴木：そうね。↘　これなんか、どうかな。↗
すずき
　　Let's see, how about this one?

田中：これ、私に読めるでしょうか。↘
　　Do you think I'll be able to read it?

鈴木：うん、基本的な概念の説明だから、だいじょうぶだと思うけど。
　　　きほんてき　がいねん　せつめい　　　　　　　　　　　　おも
　　It explains the basic concepts, so you should be all right.

田中：じゃ、読んでみます。
　　I'll try (to read it), then.　　　　　　　　　　　　　　　〈M〉

b. You can ask for further books by using the following:

ほかのは	ありませんか。↗	*Are there any others?*
	ないでしょうか。↘	

200

Ask like this if you want something in English:

A：あの、英語（で書いてある）のはないでしょうか。↘

B：そうですね。↘　ちょっと待ってください。

S-4.　How to thank for/decline offers of help

a. お手数かけて can be used to thank politely for help offered:

鈴木▽：そうそう。あと、医学の診断システムの本もたしか……。
Oh right, there was a book on diagnostic systems, too.

田中△：すみません、お手数かけて。
Sorry to trouble you.

b. To decline an offer of help politely, you can indicate that you are all right with **だいじょうぶです** or **けっこうです** followed by an explanation why you don't need help:

① 鈴木：駅まで（車で）送ろうか。
Shall I drive you to the station?

リサ：いえ、だいじょうぶです。まだバスがありますから。
ありがとうございます。
No thanks, there are still buses. Thank you.

② 学生：あの、ほかのはないでしょうか。↘
Um, do you have any others?

貸出し係：そうね。↘　ちょっと待って。
Let me see...（Looking for a book）

学生：すみません、お手数かけて。
I'm sorry to trouble you.

貸出し係：おかしいな。↘　いつもはここに置いてあるんだけど……。
How strange! It's usually placed here but...

学生：あ、じゃ、けっこうです。また来てみますから。
どうも、すみませんでした。
Thank you anyway. I'll come again.

CN

S-5. How to ask how long you can borrow something

a. When you don't know for how long you can borrow something, you can ask with the potential form of 借りる or お借りする. ⇨L18GN I

どのぐらい	借りられますか。🈓	*How long can I borrow it?*
	お借りできますか。🈓	

何日ぐらい *how many days* can be used as well:

① 学　生　：何日ぐらい借りられますか。
How many days can I borrow it?

貸出し係：2 週間です。
Two weeks.

If you ask about the deadline with いつまで, the listener will normally answer with までに (⇨L16GN Ⅳ) and 返す.

いつまで	借りられますか。🈓	*Until when can I borrow it?*
	お借りできますか。🈓🈯	

② 学　生　：いつまでお借りできますか。

貸出し係：来週の水曜日までに返してください。
Please return it by next Wednesday.

b. You can confirm the lending time as follows:

～	でしたね。↗🈓	～, *right?*
	だったね。↗🈐	

田中：ええと、2 週間でしたね。↗

鈴木：そう。

でしたね／だったね can only be used to confirm things you know, whereas
ですね／(だ) ね can be used to confirm/check things you either know or don't know.

第16課

電話をかける⑵：タクシーを呼ぶ
でんわ　　　　　　　　　　　　　　　　　　　　よ

Phoning⑵：Calling a taxi

OBJECTIVES:

GRAMMAR

Ⅰ．The -(y)oo form: the plain form of 〜ましょう
Ⅱ．〜たり、〜たりする: indicating a range of
　　　　　　　　　　　　　　activities
Ⅲ．〜し: indicating an addition
Ⅳ．の〈3〉／こと: nominalizing a sentence
Ⅴ．More on noun modification 〈3〉

CONVERSATION

＜General Information＞
1. Using a taxi

＜Strategies＞
S-1. How to propose a joint course of action
S-2. How to substantiate a point with reasons
S-3. How to call a taxi by phone
S-4. How to explain where you are
S-5. How to give instructions in a taxi

Model Conversation

(1)

Characters ： Tanaka(田中), Yamashita(山下)

Situation ： Yamashita-san is at a disco with friends. He and Tanaka-san, who are taking a break in the coffee shop on the 1st floor in the same building, realize that it's getting late, so they call a taxi.

Flow-chart ：

```
┌────────────────────────┐
│   Checking the time     │      In the coffee shop
└────────────────────────┘
            ↓
┌────────────────────────┐
│  Offering to call a taxi │
└────────────────────────┘
```

― 喫茶店で ―

田 中：ねえ、今、何時。
山 下：ええと、あ、もう11時すぎだ。
田 中：もう、バス、ないわね。
山 下：じゃ、タクシー呼ぼうか。鈴木さんもよっぱらっちゃったし。
田 中：そうね。8人だから、2台いるわね。
山 下：じゃ、ぼく、電話するよ。

(2)

Characters ： Yamashita(山下), a receptionist at the taxi company(タクシー)

Situation ： Yamashita-san calls the taxi company.

Flow-chart ：

```
┌────────────────────────┐
│ Calling the taxi company │      On the phone
└────────────────────────┘
            ↓
┌────────────────────────┐
│ Explaining the pick-up point │
└────────────────────────┘
            ↓
┌────────────────────────┐
│      Confirmation       │
└────────────────────────┘
```

― 電話（タクシー営業所） ―

タクシー：はい、やまとタクシーです。
山 下　：あ、すみません。大学の北のほうまで、2台お願いします。
タクシー：はい。

＊　　＊　　＊

タクシー：今、どちらですか。

山　下　：ええと、緑町の「ノア」という喫茶店なんですけど。

タクシー：何か、目印になるものありますか。

山　下　：ううん……。松見公園の近くなんですけど。

タクシー：ああ、緑町3丁目の交差点ね。

山　下　：ええ、その交差点を、駅からだと、左に入るんです。

タクシー：はい。

山　下　：そうすると、「タロー」というレストランがあるんですけど。

タクシー：「タロー」ね。

山　下　：ええ。その先の喫茶店です。

タクシー：はい。喫茶店の名前は。

山　下　：「ノア」です。2階がディスコになっているところなんですけど。

タクシー：あ、はい、わかりました。

＊　　＊　　＊

タクシー：お客さん、お名前は。

山　下　：あ、山下です。

タクシー：はい、山下さんですね。

山　下　：ええ。

タクシー：2台ですね。

山　下　：はい。

タクシー：じゃ、10分ぐらいで行きますから。

山　下　：じゃ、よろしくお願いします。

タクシー：はい、どうも。

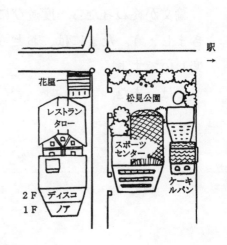

MC

Report

<山下さんの手紙>

松本くん、お元気ですか。

論文のほうはどうですか。ぼくはあまり進んでいません。

きのうの夜は、友だちといっしょにはじめてディスコに行きました。ぼくはおどりは苦手なんですが、留学生のリサさんという人がとても上手です。ぼくも教えてもらっておどってみました。けっこう楽しかったですよ。気がついたらもう11時すぎで、バスはないし、先輩の鈴木さんはよっぱらっていたし、タクシーで帰ってきました。

論文が終わったら一度遊びに来ませんか。いっしょにディスコへ行きましょう。たまには、おどったり飲んだりしてみんなでさわぐのも楽しいですよ。

では、また。

山下より

10月13日

New Words and Expressions

Words in the conversation

〜時すぎ	〜じすぎ	*after〜 o'clock*
タクシー		*taxi*
呼ぶ	よぶ	*to call (by telephone)*
よっぱらう		*to get drunk*
いる		*to need*
やまとタクシー		name of a taxi company
北	きた	*north*
〜のほう		general direction/area
緑町	みどりちょう	name of ward
ノア		name of a coffee shop
目印	めじるし	*mark, landmark*
松見公園	まつみこうえん	name of a park
〜丁目	〜ちょうめ	*〜chome*
交差点	こうさてん	*crossing, crossroads*
入る	はいる	*to turn off the main road, to enter (a side street)*
そうすると		*then, in that case*
タロー		name of a restaurant
先	さき	*ahead, beyond*
ディスコ		*disco*
お客さん	おきゃくさん	expression for addressing a customer

MC

＜Expressions in the conversation＞

鈴木さんもよっぱらっちゃったし。 *Since Suzuki-san is drunk (and besides...)*

　　〜し ⇨GNⅢ, [V-te] しまう ⇨L22GNⅡ

　　In casual speech, 〜てしまう is often contracted to 〜ちゃう and 〜てしまった to 〜ちゃった.

「ノア」という喫茶店 *a coffee shop called 'Noa'*

　　〜という〜 ⇨L11GNⅣ

何か目印になるもの   *something that serves as a landmark*

なに　めじるし

何か ⇨L15GNⅥ, ～もの ⇨GNⅥ

何か～もの indicates the idea of *something*.

駅からだと、左に入るんです。   *If (you come) from the station, turn left.*

えき　　　　ひだり　はい

　～と ⇨L12GNⅠ

2階がディスコになっているところ   *the place which has a disco on the 2nd floor.*

かい

　⇨GNⅤ

Words in the report

松本くん	まつもとくん	Yamashita's male friend
夜	よる	*night*
はじめて		*for the first time*
おどり		*dance*
苦手（な）	にがて（な）	*poor at, don't like*
おどる		*to dance*
けっこう		*quite*
楽しい	たのしい	*enjoyable, happy*
気がつく	きがつく	*to realize*
先輩	せんぱい	*one's senior*
帰る	かえる	*to go/come home*
終わる	おわる	*to be over, to finish*
一度	いちど	*once*
遊ぶ	あそぶ	*to play*
たまには		*once in a while*
みんなで		*all together*
さわぐ		*to make merry, to make a noise*

<Expressions in the report>

お元気ですか。 *How are you?*
げんき

論文のほうはどうですか。 *How about your thesis?*
ろんぶん
　　　　〜のほうは ⇨L15CN S-1

遊びに来ませんか。 *How about coming to visit?*
あそ　　き

おどったり、飲んだりして *dancing and drinking*
の
　　　　〜たり、〜たりする ⇨GNⅡ

MC

Grammar Notes

Ⅰ. The-(y)oo form: the plain form of ～ましょう

Examples

① A：いっしょに行こうか。   *Shall we go together?*

  B：ええ、いっしょに行きましょう。   *Yes, let's go together.*

② あした学校を休もうと思います。
 I'm thinking about missing school tomorrow.

③ 北海道を旅行しようと思っています。
 I'm thinking about travelling around Hokkaido.

【*Explanation*】

1. -(y)oo form: the plain form of ～ましょう

In Lesson 3, we saw the use of [V(base)] ましょう, meaning *Let's* ～ or *Shall we/I* ～? in questions, and *Let me (do)*～ in statements.

In this lesson, let us take a look at the -(y)oo form ([V-(y)oo]), which is the plain form of [V(base)] ましょう. The -(y)oo form is used in casual style conversations; in ① above, A uses the -(y)oo form, while B uses [V(base)] ましょう. ⇨CN S-1

[V(base)] ましょう	↔	-(y)oo form ([V-(y)oo])

じゃ、始めましょう。   ↔   じゃ、始めよう。   *Right, let's begin.*

A：帰りましょうか。   ↔   A：帰ろうか。   *Shall we go back?*

B：ええ、帰りましょう。 ↔   B：うん、帰ろう。   *Yes, let's (go back).*

私が払いましょう。   ↔   私が払おう。   *I'll pay. (=Let me pay).*

荷物を持ちましょう。   ↔   荷物を持とう。   *I will carry (=Let me take) your baggage.*

-(y)oo form		
	[V-(r)u] (dictionary form)	**-(y)oo** form
Group Ⅰ **-u** ↓ **-oo**	kaku　　　*to write* 書く matsu　　*to wait* 待つ hanasu　*to speak* 話す au　　　　*to meet* 会う	kakoo 書こう matoo 待とう hanasoo 話そう aoo 会おう
Group Ⅱ **-ru** ↓ **-yoo**	akeru　　*to open* 開ける neru　　　*to sleep* 寝る miru　　　*to see* 見る iru　　　*to be, stay* いる	akeyoo 開けよう neyoo 寝よう miyoo 見よう iyoo いよう
Group Ⅲ	suru　　　*to do* する kuru　　　*to come* 来る	shiyoo しよう koyoo 来よう

GN

2. [V-(y)oo]＋と思う／思っている

To express your intentions or plans, add **と思う／思っている** after the **-(y)oo** form （②③）.

1. こんばんレポートを書こうと思います。

I think I'll write the report tonight.

2. 九州を旅行しようと思っています。
きゅうしゅう　　りょこう
I am thinking of travelling around Kyushu.

Use **[V-(y)oo]＋と思う** for expressing your intentions or plans, whereas **[V-(r)u]＋と思う** can only be used to indicate someone else's plans: ⇨L11GNⅡ

3. 東京に行こうと思います。　　*I'm planning to go to Tokyo.*

4. 東京に行くと思います。　　*I think (someone) will go to Tokyo.*

Ⅱ. 〜たり、〜たりする: indicating a range of activities

Examples

① A：日曜日は何をしますか。　　*What do you do on Sundays?*

B：手紙を書いたり、本を読んだりします。　　*I write letters and read.*

② A：パーティーはどうでしたか。　　*How was the party?*

B：歌ったり、おどったりしてとても楽しかったです。
We had a good time, singing and dancing (and so on).

【*Explanation*】

　　〜たり、〜たりする indicates a range of activities; the implication is that the activities mentioned were not the only ones that took place. In ①, B mentions letter-writing and reading but implies that he does other things on Sundays, too, and in ②, lists singing and dancing as some of the things that people did at the party.

　　り is added to the plain past positive form of at least one verb, often two or more, and is normally followed by a form of する.

1. 毎日ラジオを聞いたり、テレビを見たりしています。
I am doing things like listening to the radio and watching TV.

2. 友だちに会ったり、買物したりしようと思っています。
I'm planning to meet friends and go shopping (and so on).

3. きのうはせんたくしたりして、とても忙しかった。
I was very busy yesterday doing chores like the washing.

212

Ⅲ. 〜し: indicating an addition

Examples

① **リサさんはポークも食べるし、チキンも食べます。**
Lisa-san eats both pork and chicken.

② **この会社にはコンピュータもないし、ワープロもない。**
In this company there is neither a computer nor a word processor.

③ **A：でかけませんか。**
How about going out?

B：ええ。宿題も終わったし、でかけましょう。
OK, I've finished my homework, so let's go out.

【*Explanation*】

し connects two or more states of a similar kind, in the sense of *what's more/and besides*. It can be used to characterize the topic, as in ①, where the implication may be that Lisa-san is the sort of person who will eat anything/has no strong likes and dislikes in food, or ②, where the implication may be that this company is old-fashioned or useless. Can you try to work out what the speaker wants to say in the し sentences below?

1. **鈴木さんは英語も話すし、フランス語も話します。**
Suzuki-san speaks English, and French, too.

2. **頭も痛いし、熱もあります。**
I have a headache, and a fever, too.

GN

{S₁ [plain]} し can also imply a reason for {S₂} , as in ③. Here are some more examples: ⇨CN S-2

3. きょうは天気もいいし、せんたくをしましょう。

   It is fine today, so I'll do the washing.

4. A：いっしょに出かけませんか。

   Why don't we go out together?

   B：雨が降っているし、お金もないし、きょうは出かけません。
   雨が降っているし、お金もないから、きょうは出かけません。
   雨が降っているし、お金もないし……

   It is raining and besides I have no money, so I'm (not going out.)...

も *also* is often used in these sentences to reinforce the meaning of し. Note that {S₂} takes either the plain or polite form depending on the level of formality, whereas {S₁} usually takes the plain form only.

[V]	読む 読まない 読んだ 読まなかった	
[A]	いい よくない よかった よくなかった	し、 + {S}
[NA]	元気だ 元気じゃない 元気だった 元気じゃなかった	
[N]	雨だ 雨じゃない 雨だった 雨じゃなかった	

Ⅳ. の〈3〉／こと: nominalizing a sentence

1. の and こと

Compare how the sentences (1) *Anil-san likes Japanese.* and (2) *Anil-san likes speaking Japanese.* are expressed:

	noun/noun sentence	
（1） アニルさんは	日本語	が好きです。
（2） アニルさんは	日本語を話す　の／こと	が好きです。

Attaching **の** or **こと** *(the fact) that* or *V-ing* to the end of a sentence in its plain form allows it to function like a noun:

[V]	話す 話さない 話した 話さなかった	
[A]	高い 高くない 高かった 高くなかった	
[NA]	元気な* 元気じゃない 元気だった 元気じゃなかった	＋ の こと
[N]	病気な* 病気じゃない 病気だった 病気じゃなかった	

* With [N]/[NA], [N]/[NA]な＋の is preferred to [N]/[NA]な＋こと

GN

1. **日本語を話すことはおもしろい。**
   にほんご はな
   Speaking Japanese is interesting.

2. **外国で生活するのはたいへんです。**
   がいこく せいかつ
   Living in a foreign country is tough.

3. **日本人はおふろに入るのが好きです。**
   にほんじん はい す
   Japanese like taking baths.

4. **日本語は、話すのはやさしいですが、書くのはむずかしいです。**
   か
   As for Japanese, speaking is easy, but writing is difficult.

5. **スミスさんが国に帰るのを知っていますか。**
   くに かえ し
   Do you know that Smith-san will go back home?

6. **きょう授業がないことを知りませんでした。**
   じゅぎょう
   I didn't know that there is no class today.

7. **田中さんが病気なのを知りませんでした。**
   たなか びょうき
   I didn't know that Tanaka-san was ill.

2. Differences between the use of の and こと

Generally, **の** is used more than **こと** in conversation.

1） **の** only is used in the following types of sentences:

(1) Seeing or hearing something/someone doing something.

1. **きのう田中さんが本屋に入るのを見ました。**
   ほんや はい み
   I saw Tanaka-san go into the bookshop yesterday.

2. **ゆうべ鈴木さんがきれいな女の人と歩いているのを見ましたよ。**
   すずき おんな ひと ある
   I saw Suzuki-san walking with a pretty girl last night.

3. **電話がなっているのが聞こえませんか。**
   でんわ き
   Can't you hear the telephone ringing?

(2) **の** is preferred to **こと** in sentences involving 〜が上手だ／下手だ／好きだ
   じょうず へた
   ／きらいだ／いやだ: ⇨L13GN I

1. **リサさんは日本語を話すのが上手です。**
   Lisa-san is good at speaking Japanese.

216

2. 私は歌を歌うのが下手です。
I'm hopeless at singing.

3. 雨の日に出かけるのはいやですね。
Going out on a rainy day is awful.

2）こと only is used in the following type of sentence:
　[N] は [N] です sentence.

1. 私の趣味は本を読むことです。
My hobby is reading books.

2. 好きなことは友だちと話すことです。
My favourite pastime is talking with my friends.

V．More on noun modification〈3〉

Examples

① 目印になるものがありますか。
Are there any landmarks?

(＝Is there anything which serves as a landmark?)

② 2階がディスコになっているところです。
It's the place which has a disco on the 2nd floor.

GN

【*Explanation*】

We came across noun modification in Lesson 10 and 13; let's now look at the way abstract nouns are modified in ① and ②:

①　　目印になる　　もの　　*a thing which serves as a landmark*

［目印になるもの］がありますか。

② <u>2階がディスコになっている</u>　[ところ]　*a place where the second floor is a disco*

↓

[2階がディスコになっているところ] です。

1. A：田中さんってどの人ですか。
　　Which person is Tanaka-san?

　 B：ああ、あそこでコピーをとっている人です。
　　Oh, the person (who is) making photocopies over there.

2. A：「森ビル」ってどれですか。
　　Which one is the Mori building?

　 B：あそこの、地下が駐車場になっているビルですよ。
　　It's the building over there with a car park in the basement.
　　(It's the building over there whose basement is a car park.) ⇨L13GNⅢ

Conversation Notes

<*General Information*>

1. Using a taxi

In Japan, you can take a taxi at a taxi stand near a railway station, or you can hail one on the street. You can also call a taxi by telephone. ⇨CN S-3

Taxi fares are shown on the meter, based on time and distance (for the first two kilometers, you only pay a basic fare of around ¥600), although fares can vary in different areas of Japan. There is a late night surcharge (from 11:00 p.m. to 5:00 a.m.). Tipping is not usual.

When you go to a destination that is generally known, you only need to give the driver its name, but otherwise you have to give some landmark near the destination, as in Japan it is difficult to identify a place by its address only.

<*Strategies*>

S-1. How to propose a joint course of action

You can propose a joint course of action by using the **-(y) oo** form of verbs: ⇨GN I

タクシー、 | 呼ぼうか。↘ 🌝   *Shall we call a taxi?*
            | 呼びましょうか。↘ 📧

A negative question can also be used:

タクシー、 | 呼ばない。↗ 🌝
            | 呼びませんか。↗ 📧

You can indicate agreement with the proposal as follows:

そう | ね。↗ 🌝🚹   *Yes, I agree.*
    | だね。↗ 🌝🚹
    | ですね。↗ 📧

You can show an air of decisiveness by adding そうしましょう or the -(y) oo form of the verb used in the proposal:

そうしよう。 ⓒ   *Let's do that.*
そうしましょう。 🖼

① ⓒ A：タクシー呼ぼうか。↘

    B：うん。そうしよう。

② 🖼 A🔼：そろそろ帰りませんか。↗   *Shall we go home now?*
    B🔼：そうですね。↗帰りましょう。 *Yes, let's go home.*

S-2. How to substantiate a point with reasons

You can substantiate a point with a number of reasons, adding し (⇨ GNⅢ) to each one like an afterthought:

① 🖼 A：そろそろ帰りませんか。
    仕事も終わったし、おなかもすいたし。
    Shall we go home now?
    We've finished work, and besides we're hungry.

    B：そうですね。帰りましょう。
    Yes, let's go home.

You can show only one reason as follows:

② ⓒ 山下：じゃ、タクシー呼ぼうか。
    鈴木さんもよっぱらっちゃったし。
    Well, shall we call a taxi?
    Besides, Suzuki-san is drunk.

田中：そうね。
    I agree.

S-3. How to call a taxi by phone

a. Giving your location

You indicate where you are as follows:

今＜location＞	なんですけど。 にいるんですけど。	*I'm in ＜location＞ now.*

① **タクシー：今、どちらですか。**
Where are you now?

山下：ええと、緑町の「ノア」という喫茶店なんですけど。
Um, I'm in the coffee shop Noa in Midoricho.

You can give that information without being asked first:

② **今、緑町の「ノア」という喫茶店なんですけど、大学まで２台お願いします。**

You may have to tell the driver how to get there by giving nearby landmarks.
⇨CN S-4

b. Giving your destination

When calling a taxi by phone, you indicate where you want to go:

＜destination＞まで	お願いします。 お願いしたいんですが。	*I'd like a taxi to ＜destination＞.*

CN

① **あのう、新宿駅の東口までお願いしたいんですが。**
I'd like a taxi to the east entrance of Shinjuku station.

If you need more than one car, attach **〜台** (the counter for vehicles) to the number: ⇨まとめ1AⅡ

② **大学の北のほうまで、２台お願いします。**
Two cars, please, to the north side of the university.

c. Asking how long you have to wait

If you want to find out how long you'll have to wait, you can ask:

① 客 ： 何分ぐらい ｜ で来ますか。
きゃく 　 どのぐらい

How many minutes will it take?

タクシー：10分ぐらいで行きます。
ぶん　　　い

(The taxi) will be there in about 10 minutes.

You can finish the conversation by saying よろしくお願いします.

② タクシー：お客さん、お名前は。
きゃく　　なまえ

山 下 ：あ、山下です。
やま した

タクシー：じゃ、10分ぐらいで行きますから。
ぶん　　　い

山 下 ：じゃ、よろしくお願いします。

S-4. How to explain where you are

a. Giving the nearest landmark

You can explain where you are by giving a nearby landmark, by using the following: ⇨L12CN1

＜landmark＞の近くなんですけど。 ｜ *Near ＜landmark＞.*
近くに＜landmark＞があるんですけど。 ｜ *There's ＜landmark＞*
ちか ｜ *around here.*

① タクシー：何か目印になるものありますか。
なに めじるし

Is there any sort of a landmark?

山 下 ：ううん……。松見公園の近くなんですけど。
まつみこうえん

Umm... It's near Matsumi Park.

タクシー：ああ、緑町3丁目の交差点ね。
みどりちょう ちょうめ こうさてん

Oh, the Midori-cho 3-chome crossing, right?

② タクシー：何か目印になるものは。

Any sort of a landmark?

客 ：ええと、近くに学校があるんですけど。
がっこう

Let me see... there's a school nearby here.

タクシー：ああ、緑町小学校ね。
Oh, Midori-cho elementary school, right?

b. Explaining how to get there

You can explain how to get from the first landmark to a second one in relation to the direction where the taxi comes from:

＜general direction＞からだと、　　　　　*If you come from ＜general direction＞,*

＜turning point＞を～んです。　　　　　*～ at ＜turning point＞.*

そうすると、＜landmark＞があるんですけど。　*Then you'll see ＜landmark＞.*

客　：**駅からだと、緑町3丁目の交差点を左に入るんです。**
If you come from the station, turn left at the Midori-cho 3-chome crossing.

タクシー：はい。
Yeah.

客　：**そうすると、「タロー」というレストランがあるんですけど。**
Then you'll see a restaurant called 'Taro'.

タクシー：「タロー」ね。
Right, 'Taro'.

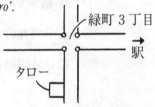

c. Explaining where you are

When the listener has taken in the last landmark, you can give your position with words indicating a relative location:

その ｛先／手前／前／となり｝（の＜place＞）です。

① **タクシー：「タロー」ね。**

　山下　：**ええ。その先の喫茶店です。**

If the last landmark is where you are, you can just say **そこです**:

② **タクシー：ああ、あの白い建物ですね。**
I see. You mean that white building, don't you?

　客　：**ええ、そこです。**

If necessary, you can add more information about the place.

③ **タクシー：喫茶店の名前は。**
なまえ

What's the name of the coffee shop?

山 下 ：**「ノア」です。2 階がディスコになっているところなんで**
かい
すけど。

It's 'Noa', the one where there is a disco on the 2nd floor.

タクシー：あ、はい、わかりました。

Oh, yes, I've got it.

S-5. How to give instructions in a taxi

In a taxi, you need to give appropriate instructions to the driver.

a. Giving your destination

When you get in a taxi, you can give your destination by using **〜までお願いします**.
ねが

① **新宿駅の東口までお願いします。**
しんじゅくえき　ひがしぐち

② **大学の北の方までお願いします。**
だいがく　きた　ほう

③ **松見公園の近くまでお願いします。**
まつみこうえん　ちか

① **東口**　　② **北の方**　　③ **近く**

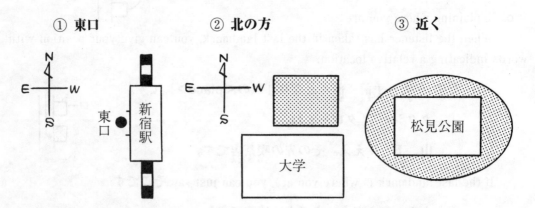

b. Indicating a turn

If necessary, you can explain where to make a turn by using **〜を右/左に曲がって**
ま
ください.

① そのかどを右に曲がってください。

② その信号を左に曲がってください。

If asked about making a turn or not, you can answer as follows:

③ タクシー：ここ、左ですか。

Left here?

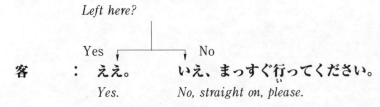

客　　　：　ええ。　　　いえ、まっすぐ行ってください。
　　　　　　Yes.　　　*No, straight on, please.*

c. Explaining where to stop

You can indicate where to stop with 〜で止めてください.

① そのビルの前で止めてください。

② その歩道橋の先で止めてください。

③ その信号の手前で止めてください。

① 前　　　　　　　② 先　　　　　　　③ 手前

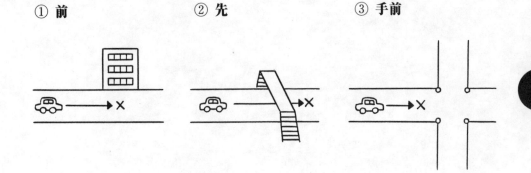

225

まとめ 4

A. GRAMMAR

Ⅰ. Complex sentences

Ⅱ. The combinations 〜てみる／〜ておく／
〜てくる／〜ている, etc.

Ⅲ.《＋を verbs》 and 《ーを verbs》

Ⅳ. が and は: は as a substitute for が, を, etc.

B. CONVERSATION

Ⅰ. Summary of Conversational Strategies

Ⅱ. Additional Information
  1. Expressions for starting a conversation
  2. Thanking for a favour

A. Grammar

Ⅰ. Complex sentences

1. Cause/Reason

1）

$\{S_1\}$	から、	$\{S_2\}$	*Because* ①, ②
cause/reason		effect/result	⇨L4GNⅢ
①		②	

1. **熱がありましたから、授業を休みました。**
   Because I had a fever, I missed the class.

2. **時間がないから、いそぎましょう。**
   Because there isn't time, let's hurry.

3. **あしたは休みだから、映画に行きます。**
   Tomorrow is a holiday, so I'll go to the movies.

2）

$\{S_1 [plain]^*\}$	ので、	$\{S_2\}$	*Because* ①, ②
cause/reason		effect/result	⇨L9GNⅢ
①		②	

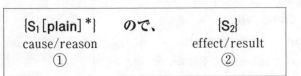

* [NA] だ ⎫ → [NA] な
  [N] だ ⎭ → [N] な

1. **熱があったので、授業を休みました。**
   Because I had a fever, I missed the class.

2. **時間がないので、いそぎましょう。**
   Because there isn't time, let's hurry.

3. **あしたは休みなので、映画に行きます。**
   Tomorrow is a holiday, so I'll go to the movies.

2. Contrast

1）

① *but/however* ②
⇨L7GNⅢ

1. **これは小さいですが、重いです。**
   It's small, but heavy.

2. **漢字の辞書を買ったけれど、使い方がわからない。**
   I bought a Kanji dictionary, but I don't know how to use it.

{S₁} can also be used as a hint implying a question you'd like to ask. {S₂} can be omitted because the listener can guess what you want to know:

3. **この漢字がわからないんですけど、（何て読むんですか）。**
   I don't know how to read this Kanji... (How do you read it?)

3. Time relations

1）

①&② shows time sequence.
① *first and then* ②
⇨L12GNⅢ

1. **おふろに入ってから、ビールを飲んだ。**
   I took a bath and then drank some beer.

2. **家に帰ってから、リサさんに電話します。**
   I'll go home and then phone Lisa-san.

2）

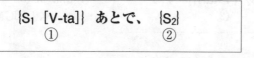

① *first and then* ②
⇨L12GNⅣ

1. **勉強したあとで、部屋をそうじした。**
   After I finished studying, I cleaned my room.

2. **先生と相談したあとで、手紙を書きたい。**
   I want to write the letter after consulting my teacher.

まとめ

229

*[N] のあとで

3. 鈴木さんは食事のあとで、ディスコに行きました。
Suzuki-san went to a disco after the meal.

3)

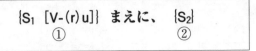

① *before* ②
② *first and then* ①
⇨L12GNV

1. 部屋をそうじするまえに、勉強した。
I studied before I cleaned my room.

2. 手紙を書くまえに、先生と相談したい。
I want to consult my teacher before I write the letter.

*[N] のまえに

3. 夏休みのまえに、テストがあります。
We will have a test before the summer vacation.

4)

① *first and then* ②
② *along* ①
⇨L6GNIV

1. きのうは、勉強して、部屋のそうじをした。
Yesterday, I studied and (then) cleaned my room.

2. 漢字をノートに書いて、覚えた。
I wrote some Kanji in the notebook and memorized them.

4. Range of activities

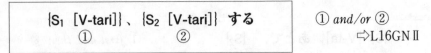

① *and/or* ②
⇨L16GNII

1. 日曜日は、泳いだり、テニスしたりする。
I spend Sundays swimming and playing tennis.

2. 毎日、ビデオを見たり、コンピュータを使ったり、漢字を書いたりする。
Everyday we do things like watching videos, using computers and writing Kanji.

5. Addition

{S₁ [plain]} し、 {S₂}
① ②

besides ①, ② *also*
⇨L16GNⅢ

1. **頭も痛いし、熱もあります。**
   あたま いた　ねつ
   I have a headache and a fever, too.

2. **お金もないし、雨も降っているし、どこへも行かない。**
   かね　あめ ふ　い
   I have no money. Besides, it's raining. So I won't go anywhere.

6. Quoting

{S [plain]}	と (って)*	言う 思う

⇨L9GNⅡ, L11GNⅡ
*って is used in the conversation.

1. **ロペスさんは夏休みに国へ帰りたいと言っています。**
   なつやす　くに かえ　い
   Lopez-san is saying that he wants to go back to his country during the summer vacation.

2. **私の先生はとてもきびしいと思います。**
   わたし せんせい　おも
   I think my teacher is very strict.

3. **田中さんはパーティーに行かないって言っていたよ。**
   た なか　い
   Tanaka-san said that she wouldn't go to the party.

7. Conditionals

まとめ

1)

{S₁ [V-tara]} 、 {S₂}
① ②

when/if ① *is realized, then* ②
⇨L11GNⅠ

1. **国に帰ったら、大学で教えたい。**
   くに かえ　だいがく おし
   When I go back to my country, I want to teach at a university.

2. **わからなかったら、田中さんに聞いてください。**
   き
   If you don't understand, please ask Tanaka-san.

3. **寒かったら、窓を閉めていいですよ。**
   さむ　まど し
   If you feel cold, you may close the window.

2)

| {S <question word>＋ [V-tara]} いいですか。 | ⇨L11GN I |

1. **あした何時に来たらいいですか。**
   なんじ　き
   What time should I come tomorrow?

2. **だれに聞いたらいいですか。**
   き
   Whom should I ask?

3)

| {S₁ [plain non-past]} と、 {S₂} | *when* ① *, naturally* ② |
| ①　　　　　　　　　　②　　　| ⇨L12GN I |

{S₂} must be a statement of fact; structures indicating intention, suggestion etc.
（～ください，～ましょう，～たい）cannot be used.

1. **冬になると、寒くなります。**
   ふゆ　　　　　さむ
   When winter comes, it gets cold.

2. **その角を曲がると、駅が見えます。**
   かど　ま　　　えき　み
   When you turn that corner, you'll find the station.

3. **学生だと、安くなる。**
   がくせい　やす
   For students it's cheaper.

8. Noun modification

| {S₁ (S₂ [plain] *＋ [N])} | ⇨L10GN I , L13GN Ⅲ, L16GN V |

* [NA] だ→ [NA] な
  [N] 　だ→ [N] 　の

1. **これは日曜日に買った本です。**
   にちようび　か　ほん
   This is a book that I bought on Sunday.

2. **まだ習っていない漢字がたくさんある。**
   なら　　　　　かんじ
   There is a lot of Kanji which I haven't learnt yet.

3. **田中さんが作った料理はおいしかった。**
   たなか　つく　りょうり
   The food which Tanaka-san cooked was delicious.

4. **2階がディスコになっているところです。**
   かい
   It's the place where the second floor is a disco.

9. Nominalizing

$$\{S_1 \; (S_2 \; [\text{plain}]^* + \text{の／こと})\}$$

⇨L16GN IV

```
* [NA] だ|      [NA] な
            → 
  [N]  だ|      [N]  な
```

1. きょう授業がないことを知りませんでした。
I didn't know that there is no class today.

2. 外国で生活するのは大変です。
Living in a foreign country is tough.

3. 私の趣味は本を読むことです。
My hobby is reading.

II. The combinations ～てみる/～ておく/～てくる/～ている, etc.

Tell the differences between a. and b. in the following sentences.

1. 1) a. このケーキを食べてください。

   b. このケーキを食べてみてください。　　　⇨L15GN I

   2) a. 新しいセーターを着ました。

   b. 新しいセーターを着てみました。

2. 1) a. 部屋をそうじします。

   b. 部屋をそうじしておきます。　　　⇨L15GN II

   2) a. まどを開けてください。

   b. まどを開けておいてください。

3. 1) a. 事務室に行ってください。

   b. 事務室に行ってきてください。　　　⇨L15GN IV

   2) a. じゃ、木村先生に聞きます。

   b. じゃ、木村先生に聞いてきます。

4. 1) a. 大学で昼ご飯を食べましょう。

   b. 大学で昼ご飯を食べていきましょう。　　　⇨L15GN IV

まとめ

2) a. アニルさんが本を借りました。

b. アニルさんが本を借りていきました。

5. 1) a. 友だちがカメラを貸しました。

b. 友だちがカメラを貸してくれました。　　　⇨L14GNⅡ

2) a. 小川先生が日本語を教えます。

b. 小川先生が日本語を教えてくださいます。

6. 1) a. お金が落ちましたよ。

b. お金が落ちていますよ。　　　⇨L8GNV

2) a. うちの前に車が止まりましたよ。

b. うちの前に車が止まっていますよ。

7. 1) a. アリさんが電気を消しました。

b. 電気が消してあります。　　　⇨L15GNⅢ

2) a. 田中さんが本に名前を書きました。

b. 本に名前が書いてあります。

Ⅲ.《＋を verbs》 and 《－を verbs》

Below are some examples of 《＋を verbs》 and 《－を verbs》

《＋を verbs》		《－を verbs》	
閉める	to close something	閉まる	to be closed, close
決める	to decide	決まる	to be decided
かける	to hang	かかる	to be hung
上げる	to raise	上がる*	to go up
下げる	to lower	下がる	to go down
止める	to stop s.th.	止まる	to stop

まぜる	to mix	まざる	to be mixed
集める	to gather s.th.	集まる	to gather
変える	to change s.th.	変わる	to change
始める	to begin s.th.	始まる	to begin
見つける	to find	見つかる	to be found
開ける	to open s.th.	開く	to be opened, open
届ける	to deliver	届く	to reach
つける	to attach s.th., turn on	つく	to attach, come on
続ける	to continue	続く	to go on/continue
入れる	to put into	入る	to enter
回す	to turn	回る*	to revolve, tour
なおす	to fix, cure	なおる	to be fixed, get well
倒す	to push over	倒れる	to fall over
よごす	to make dirty	よごれる	to become dirty
動かす	to move s.th.	動く	to move
かわかす	to dry s.th.	かわく	to dry
出す	to take out	出る*	to come out, leave
冷やす	to cool	冷える	to get cold
こわす	to break	こわれる	to get broken
起こす	to wake up	起きる	to get up
落とす	to drop s.th.	落ちる	to fall, drop
残す	to leave	残る	to remain, be left over
焼く	to burn	焼ける	to be burnt
割る	to split s.th., break s.th.	割れる	to split, break
切る	to cut	切れる	to snap, come apart
消す	to extinguish, turn off	消える	to be extinguished, go out

* See L11GN Ⅲ about 《＋を verbs》 and 《－を verbs》. The verbs with * take を as a particle, but note that を is not the object particle を.

Ⅳ. 🐟 **が and は: は as a substitute for が，を, etc.**

Look at the cartoon. The husband is looking for today's newspaper. He can't find it, so he asks his wife 「**きょうの新聞は。**」 *Where is today's newspaper?* His wife might reply in several ways:

1. **知りませんよ。**
   I have no idea.

2. **テーブルの上にありますよ。**
   It's on the table.

3. **たろうが読んでいますよ。**
   Taro is reading it.

4. **さっき、たろうが持っていきましたよ。**
   Taro took it away a little earlier.

5. **まだ来ていませんよ。**
   It hasn't come yet.

Being the topic of the conversation, **きょうの新聞** is typically omitted in the wife's answers in Japanese, whereas it is expressed as *'it'* in the English translation.

The wife could also answer repeating the topic:

1. **新聞は、知りませんよ。**

2. **新聞は、テーブルの上にありますよ。**

3. **新聞は、たろうが読んでいますよ。**

4. **新聞は、さっきたろうが持っていきましたよ。**

5. **新聞は、まだ来ていませんよ。**

漫画（まんが）

まとめ

B. Conversation

I . *Summary of Conversational Strategies*

1. Factual information

☐ ☐ How to confirm what you heard ： ～んだって。↗／ですって。↗
from someone   ⇨L13 S-2   ～と聞きましたが。📧

☐ ☐ How to answer questions ⇨L14 S-2 ： ～です。

☐ ☐ How to confirm information —3.   ： ～です ｜ か。↗
                ⇨L14 S-3   ｜ ね。↗

☐ ☐ How to describe something ⇨L14 S-4 ： ＜shape/colour/size＞です。

☐ ☐ How to ask for advice on books ： ～について何かありますか。
                ⇨L15 S-3   ～について探しているんですけど。

☐ ☐ How to ask how long you can ： どのぐらい ｜ お借りできますか。
borrow something   ⇨L15 S-5   いつまで ｜

☐ ☐ How to explain where you are ： ＜landmark＞の近くなんですけど。
                ⇨L16 S-4

2. Judgement

☐ ☐ How to apologize and give an excuse ： ｜S₁｜ ｜ものですから ｜、｜S₂｜
                ⇨L13 S-1   ｜ので

☐ ☐ How to substantiate a point with ： 仕事も終わったし、おなかもすいたし、
reasons   ⇨L16 S-2

3. Emotions

☐ ☐ How to express someone's feelings ： ああ、よかった。
                ⇨L14 S-5   ええっ、こまったな。

4. Actions

☐ ☐ How to apologize   ⇨L13 S-1 ： ＜reason＞て、 ｜ ごめん。
                              ｜ すみません。
                              ｜ 申しわけありません。

☐ ☐ How to make an offers   ⇨L13 S-3 ： ～てもいい。🎧
                              ～てあげましょうか。📧

☐ ☐ How to enquire about something you ： ～に忘れ物をしたんですが、
left behind   ⇨L14 S-1   ｜ ～ていただけますか。
                                ｜ ～くださいませんか。

☐ ☐ How to ask for advice on books ： ～について何かありませんか。
                ⇨L15 S-3   探しているんですけど。

☐ ☐ How to thank for/decline offers of : すみません。お手数かけて。
help ⇨L15 S-4 ーだいじょうぶです/けっこうです。

☐ ☐ How to propose a joint course of : タクシー ｜ 呼ぼうか。↘
action ⇨L16 S-1 ｜ 呼びませんか。↗
ーそうね。／そうだね。／そうですね。

☐ ☐ How to call a taxi by phone : ＜place to go＞までお願いします。
⇨L16 S-3

☐ ☐ How to give instructions in a taxi : ＜place＞を～に曲ってください。
⇨L16 S-5 ＜place＞で止めてください。

5. Social formulas

☐ ☐ How to accept an offer ⇨L13 S-4 : よろしいんですか／いいんですか。
じゃ、えんりょなく

☐ ☐ How to express modesty ⇨L13 S-5 : いいえ、｜ そんなことないですよ。
｜ それほどでも。

☐ ☐ Greeting someone you haven't met : ひさしぶり ｜ ですね。
for long time ⇨L15 S-1 しばらく ｜
ごぶさたしています。

☐ ☐ Talking about how one's getting on : どう／いかがですか。
⇨L15 S-1 ーおかげさまで。なんとか。

☐ ☐ How to talk about others ⇨L15 S-2 : ～さんは、｜ どうしてますか。
｜ どうしてる。↗
ー～って言っていました。

☐ ☐ How to thank for/decline offers of : すみません、お手数かけて。
help ⇨L15 S-4

6. Communication strategies

☐ ☐ How to confirm what you head from : ＜rumour＞ ｜ んだって。↗
someone ⇨L13 S-2 ｜ んですって。↗
｜ と聞きましたが。

☐ ☐ How to bring up the main the topic : ところで、～
⇨L13 S-3

☐ ☐ How to start a conversation —6. : おひさしぶりです(ね)。
After not having seen each other for お元気ですか。
a long time ⇨L15 S-1 ーええ、おかげさまで。

II. *Additional Information*

1. Expressions for starting a conversation

　　　When you meet someone, you can use a variety of greetings depending on the situation. Can you remember how to start a conversation?

（1）Meeting someone for the first time at a party 　　　　　　　　〈L1〉

　　　A：はじめまして。＜name＞です。どうぞよろしく。

　　　B：こちらこそ。どうぞよろしく。

（2）Meeting an acquaintance on the street 　　　　　　　　　　　〈L2〉

　　　A：｜おはよう（ございます）。　｜どちらへ。↗
　　　　｜こんにちは。　　　　　　　｜どこ行くの。↗
　　　　｜こんばんは。

　　　B：ちょっと＜place＞まで。

（3）Asking for attention at an office, a shop, etc. 　〈L2,L3,L4,L9,L10,L11〉

　　　A：｜すみません。
　　　　｜お願いします。

　　　B：はい。

（4）Asking a stranger a question 　　　　　　　　　　　　　　〈L5, L12〉

　　　A：｜あの、ちょっとすみません。
　　　　｜あのう、お願いします。

　　　B：はい。

（5）Visiting someone's room 　　　　　　　　　　　　　　　　　〈L8〉

　　　A：（knock-knock）失礼します。

　　　B：｜やあ。♂ ☻
　　　　｜あら。♀ ☻
　　　　｜こんにちは。／etc.

（6）Asking permission〈L8〉

A：ちょっと | よろしいですか。🈂️⬆️
いいですか。🈂️⬆️➡️
いいかな。↘️🄲➡️⬇️
いい。↗️🄲➡️⬇️

B： | どうぞ。
あ、今はちょっと……。↘️

（7）Meeting a casual acquaintance〈L2,L13〉

やあ。♂ | おはよう。 *Good morning.*
あら。♀ | こんにちは。 *Good afternoon.*
こんばんは。 *Good evening.*
ひさしぶり。
しばらく。 *I haven't seen you for a long time.*

（8）Being late for a meeting〈L13〉

A： | ごめん、ごめん。遅くなっちゃって。🄲
すみません、遅くなりまして。🈂️
申しわけありません、遅くなりまして。🈂️

B：いいえ。

2. Thanking for a favour

When you ask someone who is a busy person（most Japanese are!）to do you a favour,「すみません、お忙しいのに。」(*Sorry for taking up your valuable time.*) is a useful expression.「すみません。」can express thanks, and「すみません、お忙しいのに。」 is used before or after someone does something for you. Note that you don't use「ありがとう。」in this situation.

① A：あした来ていただけないでしょうか。 *Could you come tomorrow?*

B：ああ、いいですよ。

A：すみません。お忙しいのに。

B：いえ。かまわないんですよ。 *That's all right.*

まとめ

241

② A：来週、手伝っていただけないでしょうか。
　　　　らいしゅう　　てつだ

　B：ああ、いいですよ。

（After a week）

　B：こんにちは。手伝いに来ました。
　　　　　　　　　　　き

　A：すみません。お忙しいのに。
　　　　　　　　　　いそが

　B：いえ。かまわないんですよ。

Instead of **お忙しいのに**, **わざわざ** (*take the trouble to*) can be used with **すみません**, but also with **ありがとう**:

わざわざすみません。　　　　　　　　　　*Thank you for your trouble.*
わざわざありがとう（ございます）。

Appendix

I. Grammar Check

II. Answers to Grammar Check and
   Model Conversation Check

I. Grammar Check

Grammar Check L9

Read the Grammar Notes of Lesson 9, and check how well you have understood. Choose <u>the most appropriate statement</u>.

1　a）　山下さんは熱がありますを言いました。
　　b）　　　　　　　　ありますと
　　c）　　　　　　　　あるを
　　d）　　　　　　　　あると

2　a）　のどが痛いので、　病院に行きます。
　　b）　のどが痛いなので、病院に行きます。
　　c）　病院に行くので、　のどが痛いです。

3　a）　このアパートは新しいときれいです。
　　b）　　　　　　　　新しくて
　　c）　　　　　　　　新しいで

4　a）　あしたは日曜日と　授業がありません。
　　b）　　　　　　　日曜日くて
　　c）　　　　　　　日曜日で

5　a）　先生、このビデオ、見ましたか。
　　b）　　　　　　　　　　ごらんなりましたか。
　　c）　　　　　　　　　　ごらんになりましたか。

6　a）　先生がそうおっしゃいました。
　　b）　　　　　　　　おっしゃりました。

7　a）　名前を書いてだけしてください。
　　b）　名前だけ書いてください。
　　c）　だけ名前を書いてください。

8　a）　部屋をきれいになりました。
　　b）　部屋が
　　c）　部屋に

9　a）　このカメラ、もう少し安くにしてください。
　　b）　　　　　　　　　安いに
　　c）　　　　　　　　　安く

Grammar Check L10

Read the Grammar Notes of Lesson 10, and check how well you have understood. Choose <u>the most appropriate statement.</u>

1 　a）　リサさんはまじめ　学生です。
　　b）　　　　　　まじめな学生
　　c）　　　　　　まじめの学生

2 　a）　大きい　サイズのセーターをください。
　　b）　大きいなサイズ
　　c）　大きいのサイズ

3 　a）　Q：リサさんはだれ　　ですか。
　　b）　　　　　　　どの人
　　c）　　　　　　　どんな人
　　　　A：親切な人です。

4 　a）　リサさんと田中さんと、だれが　年上ですか。
　　b）　　　　　　　　　　　どれが
　　c）　　　　　　　　　　　どちらが

5 　　　Q：この中でどれが一番いいですか。
　　a）　A：これです。
　　b）　　　これがです。
　　c）　　　これのほうがいいです。

6 　a）　これは難しいので、もっとかんたんが　　読みたいです。
　　b）　　　　　　　　　　　　かんたんのが
　　c）　　　　　　　　　　　　かんたんなのが

7 　a）　先生、このコンピュータ、　使いになりますか。
　　b）　　　　　　　　　　お使いになりますか。
　　c）　　　　　　　　　　お使うになりますか。

8 　a）　家内っていうのは、奥さんのことです。
　　b）　家内ていうのは、

9 　a）　東京は物価で高いです。
　　b）　　　　物価が
　　c）　　　　物価の

245

Grammar Check L11

Read the Grammar Notes of Lesson 11, and check how well you have understood. Choose <u>the most appropriate statement.</u>

1　a）　かぜをひいたら、薬を飲んでください。
　　b）　　　　ひいて、
　　c）　　　　ひいた、

2　a）　テストがないたら、映画を見ます。
　　b）　　　　　なかったら、
　　c）　　　　　なくて、

3　a）　かばんは見つかりますを思います。
　　b）　　　　見つかりますと
　　c）　　　　見つかるを
　　d）　　　　見つかると

4　a）　ドアを開けました。
　　b）　ドアを開きました。
　　c）　ドアが開きました。

5　a）　リサさんはパスポートを落としました。
　　b）　　　　　　　　　　　落ちました。
　　c）　　　　　　　　　　　落ちています。

6　a）　『おもしろい物理』　いう本を注文します。
　　b）　　　　　　　　　の本
　　c）　　　　　　　　　という本

7　a）　本は1週間が来ます。
　　b）　　　1週間で
　　c）　　　1週間

8　a）　駅まで10分がかかります。
　　b）　　　　10分で
　　c）　　　　10分

9　a）　1か月に2度に電話をします。
　　b）　1か月に2度
　　c）　1か月　2度に

246

Grammar Check L12

Read the Grammar Notes of Lesson 12, and check how well you have understood. Choose <u>the most appropriate statement.</u>

1　a）まっすぐ行くと、　白いビルが見えます。
　　b）　　　　　行きと、
　　c）　　　　　行ったと、

2　a）食事が終わって、　コーヒーを飲みましょう。
　　b）　　　　終わると、
　　c）　　　　終わったら、

3　a）時間がありませんから、バスで行ってのほうがいいですよ。
　　b）　　　　　　　　　　　　　　　　行ったのほう
　　c）　　　　　　　　　　　　　　　　行ったほう

4　　　Q：どこで食べましょうか。
　　a）　A：うちに帰る　から、食べましょう。
　　b）　　　　　帰って
　　c）　　　　　帰った

5　a）おふろを出るあとで、ジュースを飲みます。
　　b）　　　　　出て
　　c）　　　　　出た

6　a）研究室に行く　まえに、電話をしました。
　　b）　　　　行って
　　c）　　　　行った

7　a）この電車は東京駅に通ります。
　　b）　　　　　東京駅を
　　c）　　　　　東京駅で

8　a）となりの部屋から音楽が聞こえます。
　　b）　　　　　　　音楽を聞こえます。
　　c）　　　　　　　音楽を聞きます。

9　a）先生に　　　　行ってください。
　　b）先生のところに
　　c）先生ところに

Grammar Check L13

Read the Grammar Notes of Lesson 13, and check how well you have understood.
Choose <u>the most appropriate statement</u>.

1　a）田中さんは音楽を好きです。
　　b）　　　　　音楽が
　　c）　　　　　音楽に

2　a）リサさんは私に本をあげました。
　　b）　　　　　　　　さしあげました。
　　c）　　　　　　　　くれました。

3　a）私は先生に本をくれました。
　　b）　　　　　　　くださいました。
　　c）　　　　　　　いただきました。

4　a）私はアニルさんに本をあげました。
　　b）私はアニルさんに本をくれました。
　　c）アニルさんは私に本をもらいました。

5　a）これは写真パーティーでとったです。
　　b）　　　　　パーティーでとりました写真です。
　　c）　　　　　パーティーでとったの写真です。
　　d）　　　　　パーティーでとった写真です。

6　a）すわっているあそこにの人を知っていますか。
　　b）あそこにすわっているの人
　　c）あそこにすわっている人

7　a）いま雨が降ります。
　　b）　　　　降っています。

8　a）まだ日本へ来てばかりなので、よくわかりません。
　　b）　　　　来たばかり
　　c）　　　　来るばかり

9　a）アニルさんは毎日コーヒーを１０ぱいも飲みます。
　　b）　　　　　　　　　　　　　１０ぱいで
　　c）　　　　　　　　　　　　　１０ぱいを

248

Read the Grammar Notes of Lesson 14, and check how well you have understood.
Choose <u>the most appropriate statement.</u>

1　a）　朝5時に起きられます
　　b）　あさ じ　お　起けます。
　　c）　　　　　起きできます。

2　a）　漢字をわかります。
　　b）　かんじ　漢字に
　　c）　漢字が

3　a）　きのう田中さんが（私に）電話をしました。
　　b）　たなか　　　わたし　でんわ　　　してあげました。
　　c）　　　　　　　　　　　　　してくれました。

4　a）　友だちが私の自転車をなおしました。
　　b）　とも　　　じてんしゃ　なおしてあげました。
　　c）　　　　　　　　　　　なおしてくれました。

5　a）　友だちが（私の）アパートをさがしてもらいました。
　　b）　友だちに
　　c）　友だちを

6　　　私は田中さんに本を買ってもらいました。
　　　　Q：だれが本を買いましたか。
　　a）　　私
　　b）　　田中さん

7　a）　母がセーターを送ってくれました。
　　b）　はは　　おく　　　くださいました。

8　a）　友だちと山で遊びに行きます。
　　b）　やま あそ い　山へ
　　c）　　　　山を

9　a）　6時35分に出かけるので、6時半までに終わりましょう。
　　b）　じ ふん で　　　　6時半まで　　　お
　　c）　　　　　　　　　6時半

249

Read the Grammar Notes of Lesson 15, and check how well you have understood.
Choose <u>the most appropriate statement.</u>

1　　　Q：カメラがこわれたんだけど、なおせる。
a)　A：ええ、よくわからないけど、やります。
b)　　　　　　　　　　　　　　　　やってみます。

2　a)　電気を消しておきます。
b)　　　　消えて

3　　　Q：まどが開いていますよ。
a)　A：ええ、暑いので、開いているんです。
b)　　　　　　　　　　　　　開けてあるんです。

4　a)　先生に会うまえに、電話をしています。
b)　　　　　　　　　　　　　してあります。
c)　　　　　　　　　　　　　しておきます。

5　　　Q：田中さん、いらっしゃいますか。
a)　A：となりの部屋にいるので、呼びます。
b)　　　　　　　　　　　　　呼んできます。
c)　　　　　　　　　　　　　呼んでいきます。

6　　　Q：この辞書、だれのですか。
a)　A：名前が書いてありませんか。
b)　　　名前を書いておきませんか。
c)　　　名前を書いてみませんか。

7　　　A：暑いですね。
a)　B：ええ、何を飲みませんか。
b)　　　　　　何も
c)　　　　　　何か

8　a)　あっちへ行く。
b)　　　　行こ。
c)　　　　行け。

9　a)　映画は好きじゃないので、あまり見ません。
b)　　　　　　　　　　　　　　　見ます。
c)　　　　　　　　　　　　　　　見ています。

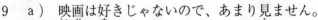

250

Read the Grammar Notes of Lesson 16, and check how well you have understood.
Choose <u>the most appropriate statement.</u>

1   A ：リサさん、休みはどうしますか。
   a） リサ：国に帰りますと思います。
   b）   帰って
   c）   帰ろう

2   a） 父が早く寝ろうと言いました。
   b）   寝ろ
   c）   寝れ

3   a） ワープロは安いし便利ですし、買おうと思っている。
   b）   便利だし、
   c）   便利し、

4   a） 雨も降っているし、きょうは行きたいです。
   b）   行きたくないです。

5   a） きのうはパーティーで食べたり飲んで、　楽しかった。
   b）   食べたし飲んで、
   c）   食べたり飲んだりして、

6   a） ひとりでいるのが　好きです。
   b）   いますのが
   c）   いるが

7   a） リサさんが走っているの　を見ました。
   b）   走っていること

8   a） 木村ビルは2階に喫茶店があることです。
   b）   あるところです。
   c）   あるです。

II. Answers to Grammar Check and Model Conversation Check

1. Answers to Grammar Check

L9	1. d	2. a	3. b	4. c	5. c	6. a	7. b	8. b	9. c
L10	1. b	2. a	3. c	4. c	5. a	6. c	7. b	8. a	9. b
L11	1. a	2. b	3. d	4. c	5. a	6. c	7. b	8. c	9. b
L12	1. a	2. c	3. c	4. b	5. c	6. a	7. b	8. a	9. b
L13	1. b	2. c	3. c	4. a	5. d	6. c	7. b	8. b	9. a
L14	1. a	2. c	3. c	4. c	5. b	6. b	7. a	8. b	9. a
L15	1. b	2. a	3. b	4. c	5. b	6. a	7. c	8. c	9. a
L16	1. c	2. b	3. b	4. b	5. c	6. a	7. a	8. b	

2. Answers to Model Conversation Check

L9	I.	1. b	2. b	3. c	4. c	5. a
	II.	1. a	2. b	3. c	4. a	5. a
L10	I.	1. b	2. c	3. a	4. b	5. c
	II.	1. a	2. c	3. c	4. b	5. b
L11	I.	1. b	2. a	3. b	4. c	5. c
	II.	1. b	2. a	3. b	4. c	5. a
L12	I.	1. a	2. a	3. a	4. b	5. a
	II.	1. b	2. c	3. b	4. c	5. a
L13	I.	1. b	2. a	3. a	4. c	5. a
	II.	1. a	2. a	3. b	4. c	5. b
L14	I.	1. b	2. c	3. c	4. a	5. b
	II	1. b	2. c	3. a	4. c	5. b
L15	I.	1. a	2. c	3. a	4. b	5. b
	II.	1. c	2. b	3. c	4. c	5. a
L16	I.	1. c	2. a	3. b	4. c	5. b
	II.	1. a	2. a	3. c	4. b	5. b

Index to Grammar Notes（L1~L16）

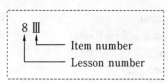

```
8 III
  ↑  ↑
  |  └── Item number
  └───── Lesson number
```

254

255

Index to Conversation Notes (L1~L16)

~て、<location>です。
~と、<location>にあります。
<shape/colour/size etc.>です。   L14S-4
<landmark>の近くなんですけど。   L15S-5

Confirming information
    ………ですか。／………ですね。   L4S-4ab
    事務室って、宿舎の事務室ですか。   L5S-3
    52の3181じゃありませんか。   L7S-3
    右に曲がると、歩道橋があります。   L12S-3
    ─右に曲がるんですね。↗
    ~んだって。↗／ですって。↗   L13S-2
    ~ですか。／ですね。↗   L14S-3

Saying something is correct
    はい。／ええ。／うん。   L1GI3

Saying something is not correct
    いいえ。   L1GI3
    あのう、おつり、ちがっているんですけど。   L2GI3c
    あのう、これちがっているんですけど。   L3S-4c
    いいえ、ちがいます。   L7S-3

Correcting someone
    いいえ、ちがいます。うちは山田ですけど。   L7S-3
    ここですか。
    ──いや、そこじゃなくて、こっち。   L9S-3

Reporting something
    事務室に取りにきてくださいって。   まとめ2BⅡ5b

Judgement

Asking permission
    ~ても／~なくてもいいでしょうか。   L9S-2

Asking for someone's judgement
    [N]は私には、[A/NA]でしょうか。   L10S-2
    [N1]と[N2]とどちらがいいでしょうか。   L10S-2
    <group>の中でどれが一番いいかな。   L10S-2

Giving reasons
    ｛S1｝｜ものですから｜、｛S2｝   L13S-1
            ｜ので｜
    仕事も終わったし、おなかもすいたし、   L16S-1

Emotion

Expressing someone's feelings   L14S-5
    ああ、よかった。
    ええっ、こまったな。

Offering to do something for someone

Nと呼んでください。 L1S-2c

これ、おねがいします。 L2S-1a

<thing>を<number> │ お願いします。 L2S-4
                    │ ください。

これでおねがいします。 L2GI3a

こちらへどうぞ。 L3GI2a

もう少し待ってください。 L3S-4a

まだですか。 L3S-4b

Nの電話番号教えてください。 L7S-1a

<shape/colour/size>の［N］を見せてください。 L10S-1

注文お願いします。 L11S-2

悪いんですけど、注文取り消してください。 L11S-3

～てあげてもいいよ。／～てあげてもいいよ。 L13S-3

タクシー呼ぼうか。／呼びましょうか。 L16S-1

<place>までお願いします。 L16S-3

<place>を～に曲がってください。 L16S-5

<place>で止めてください。 L16S-5

Giving something

はい。 L2S-1

どうぞ。 L3S-2

Receiving something

あ、どうも。 L3S-2

よろしいんですか。／じゃ、えんりょなく。 L13S-4

Asking for instructions

………が分からないんですけど。 L6S-2a

Checking what you have done

これでいいですか。 L6S-2b

Asking permission

あの、………で(も)いいですか。 L6S-5b

<reason>んです。……てもよろしいでしょうか。 L8S-3a

<reason>んです。～V-たいんですが。／ですけど。 L8S-3a

～ても／～なくてもいいでしょうか。 L9S-2

Giving permission

いいですよ。／かまいませんよ。 L8S-3c

Refusing permission

～Vではだめです。／いけません。 L8S-3c

～Vないでください。 L8S-3c

Asking for advice

ええと、はんこもってないんですけど。 L6S-4

～について何かありませんか。 L15S-1

Giving an alternative

じゃ、………でもいいです。／けっこうです。 L6S-5a

Warning someone
　　　～Ｖないでください。 ... L8S-4a

Suggesting
　　　じゃ、………はどう。↗／どうですか。 ... L6S-5a

Enquiring for something
　　　～に忘れものしたんですが、～ていただけませんか。 ... L14S-1

Making an appointment
　　　じゃ、＜time/date＞にお願いします。 ... L7S-6a
　　　いつがよろしいでしょうか。 ... L7S-6b
　　　＜time/date＞は、どうでしょうか。 ... L7S-6c

Social formulas

Introducing yourself
　　　はじめまして。[Ｎ]ともうします。
　　　どうぞよろしくお願いします。 ... L1GI1a

Introducing someone
　　　こちら、[Ｎ]さんです。 ... L1S-2b

Answering an introduction
　　　[Ｎ]です。よろしくお願いします。 ... L1S-2b

Starting a conversation with a stranger
　　　あのう、失礼ですが。 ... L1GI2b
　　　どちらへ。／どこ行くの。 ... L2S-1a
　　　すみません。 ... L2S-2
　　　失礼します。 ... L8S-1a
　　　ちょっとよろしいでしょうか。 ... L8S-1b

Expressing politeness
　　　お／ご[Ｎ] ... L1GI1b

Expressing modesty
　　　いいえ、そんなことないですよ。／それほどでも。 ... L13S-5

Greetings
　　　こんにちは。
　　　いらっしゃいませ。 ... L3GI2a
　　　ひさしぶりですね。／しばらく。／ごぶさたしています。 ... L15S-1

Talking about how one's getting on
　　　どうですか。／いかがですか。 ... L15S-1
　　　－おかげさまで。／なんとか。

Talking about others
　　　～さんは、どうしていますか。 ... L15S-2

Thanking
　　　どうも。／ごちそうさまでした。 ... 3S-5b
　　　ありがとうございます。 ... まとめ1BⅡ4
　　　──いいえ、どういたしまして。
　　　どうもすみません。 ... まとめ1BⅡ4c

すみません。お手数をかけて。   L15S-3
Apologizing
　　＜reason＞て、ごめん。／すみません。／申し訳ありません。   L13S-1
Declining politely
　　ううん………／ちょっと。～のほうがいいんですけど。   L10S-3

Communication strategies

Getting someone's attention
　　あ（ああ）／あら   まとめ1BⅡ3a
　　あ（あのう）   まとめ1BⅡ3b
Aizuchi
　　はい。／ええ。／そうですね。／そうですか。   L1GI4
Starting a conversation
　　あ、［N］さん。こんにちは。   L1S-1
　　ちょっと。／ちょっと、すみません。   L1S-1c
　　あの、ちょっとすみません。   L4S-1
　　あの、ちょっとうかがいますが。   L4S-1
　　もしもし。   L7S-2
　　あの、ちょっとおたずねしたいんですが。   L7S-4
Ending a conversation
　　じゃ、失礼します。   L2S-1b
　　ちょっと、そこまで。
　　どうも ｜ ありがとうございました。   L4S-6a
　　　　　 ｜ すみませんでした。
　　じゃ、いいです。   L5S-5
　　じゃ、よろしくお願いします。   L7S-6d
Introducing a main topic
　　掲示板にこれがはってあったんですけど。   L5S-1
　　………のことなんですが。／けど。実は、   L8S-2
Changing the topic
　　ところで、＜the main topic＞   L13S-2
Summing up
　　じゃ、コーヒーふたつ、紅茶ひとつください。   L3S-3c
Saying something again
　　すみません、もういちどお願いします。   L4S-3a
Checking that you have understood
　　じどうはんばいき。――じどう………   L4S-3b
　　事務室って、宿舎の事務室ですか。   L5S-3
Showing you do not understand
　　え。↗／はあ。↗   L4S-3c
Gaining time to collect your thoughts
　　せんたく機はどこでしょう。――せんたく機（ね）。   L4S-5a
　　ええと。   L4S-5c

Compiled and Edited by:

General editor	Otsubo, Kazuo	大坪 一夫
Authors	Akutsu, Satoru	阿久津　智
	Ichikawa, Yasuko	市 川 保 子
	Emura, Hirofumi	江 村 裕 文
	Ogawa, Taeko	小 川 多恵子
	Kano, Chieko	加 納 千恵子
	Kaiser, Stefan	カイザー シュテファン
	Kindaichi, Kyoko	金田一 京 子
	Kobayashi, Noriko	小 林 典 子
	Komiya, Shutaro	小 宮 修太郎
	Saegusa, Reiko	三 枝 令 子
	Sakai, Takako	酒 井 たか子
	Shimizu, Yuri	清 水 百 合
	Shinya, Ayuri	新 谷 あゆり
	Tochigi, Yuka	栃 木 由 香
	Tomura, Kayo	戸 村 佳 代
	Nishimura, Yoshimi	西 村 よしみ
	Hashimoto, Yoji	橋 本 洋 二
	Fujimaki, Kikuko	藤 牧 喜久子
	Ford, Junko	フォード 順子
	Homma, Tomoko	本 間 倫 子
	Yamamoto, Sonoko	山 本 そのこ
	Yokoyama, Noriko	横 山 紀 子
	Watanabe, Keiko	渡 辺 恵 子
Cover design	Robles, Maria Elizabeth	ロブレスM.エリザベス
Illustrator	Teshigahara, Midori	勅使河原　緑

SITUATIONAL FUNCTIONAL JAPANESE
VOLUME 2: NOTES

1992年 3 月13日　　初　版第 1 刷発行
1994年 4 月20日　　第 2 版第 1 刷発行
2000年 8 月25日　　第 2 版第 5 刷発行

著　者　　筑波ランゲージグループ

発行所　　株式会社　凡 人 社
　　　　　〒102－0093 東京都千代田区平河町 1 － 3 －13
　　　　　菱進平河町ビル 1 F　電話 03－3263－3959

	-(r)u f. (dic f.)	-nai f.	-ta f.	-nakatta f.	[V(base)]-masu	-te f.	-nakute f.	-tara
Group I	行く	行かない	行った	行かなかった	行きます	行って	行かなくて	行ったら
	書く	書かない	書いた	書かなかった	書きます	書いて	書かなくて	書いたら
	急ぐ	急がない	急いだ	急がなかった	急ぎます	急いで	急がなくて	急いだら
	飲む	飲まない	飲んだ	飲まなかった	飲みます	飲んで	飲まなくて	飲んだら
	死ぬ	死なない	死んだ	死ななかった	死にます	死んで	死ななくて	死んだら
	呼ぶ	呼ばない	呼んだ	呼ばなかった	呼びます	呼んで	呼ばなくて	呼んだら
	帰る	帰らない	帰った	帰らなかった	帰ります	帰って	帰らなくて	帰ったら
	待つ	待たない	待った	待たなかった	待ちます	待って	待たなくて	待ったら
	使う	使わない	使った	使わなかった	使います	使って	使わなくて	使った
	話す	話さない	話した	話さなかった	話します	話して	話さなくて	話した
Group II	食べる	食べない	食べた	食べなかった	食べます	食べて	食べなくて	食べた
	開ける	開けない	開けた	開けなかった	開けます	開けて	開けなくて	開けた
	見る	見ない	見た	見なかった	見ます	見て	見なくて	見たら
	いる	いない	いた	いなかった	います	いて	いなくて	いたら
Group III	来る	来ない	来た	来なかった	来ます	来て	来なくて	来たら
	持ってくる	持ってこない	持ってきた	持ってこなかった	持ってきます	持ってきて	持ってこなくて	持ってきたら
	する	しない	した	しなかった	します	して	しなくて	したら
	準備する	準備しない	準備した	準備しなかった	準備します	準備して	準備しなくて	準備し